PALLANT HOUSE:

ITS ARCHITECTURE, HISTORY AND OWNERS

ACKNOWLEDGEMENTS

The cost of publishing this booklet has been largely funded by donations from private individuals; without this most welcome and generous support, our budget would not allow such vital projects to go ahead. The Trustees are therefore most grateful to an anonymous Friend of Pallant House, Percy Cartwright Esq, A.H.J. Green Esq, Clive Harrison Esq, Crispin Thomas Esq, Mrs. C. Woollings and to Geoffrey Osborne Ltd.

The Trustees are also extremely grateful to Sibylla Jane Flower, a historian and descendent of the Peckham family, who has been researching the Peckhams for some years. The chapter on Henry Peckham is a part of the fruits of this research, most kindly donated for this publication. It is hoped that we can publish her history of the wider Peckham family in due course. For the chapter on the garden, the Trustees approached the acknowledged expert on the subject, Sir Roy Strong, who found the time in a very busy schedule to produce the 'green' section of this book.

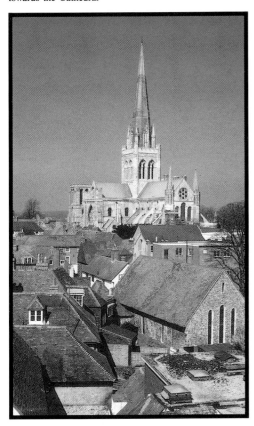

The view from the roof of Pallant House, looking towards the Cathedral

INTRODUCTION

Once a private residence, more recently local government offices and now a restored historic house and art gallery open to the public, Pallant House is one of the finest examples of domestic town architecture in England.

The derivation of the name Pallant, which applies to the whole south-east quarter of the city within the walls, is uncertain. In legal documents, a fenced or enclosed area was called a *palenta*, and enclosures would certainly have been maintained in this part of the city to contain the livestock coming into town on Tuesday evenings to await the Wednesday market held in East Street. Pallant appears as a street name in other towns, and is also an English surname. The late Latin term *Palentia* signifies an area with exclusive jurisdiction, distinct from its surroundings. This could well apply to the Pallant, which was owned and administered by the Archbishops of Canterbury until 1552.

The Pallant, a reproduction in miniature of the city itself, consists of four narrow streets meeting at a crossroads. It was here, on the site of an old malthouse, and amongst the tanneries and brewhouses of the industrial quarter, that a young merchant, Henry "Lisbon" Peckham, and his bride chose to build their new home in 1712/13. This house, built at a time when the beginnings of a national style were taking the place of the old regional vernacular styles, was to be in stark contrast to the earlier houses in the city with their wattle-and-daub walls, earth floors, thatched roofs and leaded windows.

Successive private owners lived in the house throughout the eighteenth and nineteenth centuries until 1919, when it was purchased by the Rural District Council.

After almost sixty years of use as council offices, the future of Pallant House hung in the balance. The idea of its conversion as an art gallery had already been discussed and rejected some years before, when, in 1977, the retiring Dean of Chichester, Dr. Walter Hussey, proposed the bequest to Chichester of his private collection of pictures and sculpture, if the city could find an appropriate home for it. His wish for the collection to be shown in a domestic setting, and the growing movement within the city to press for the restoration and opening of Pallant House coincided; the eventual acceptance by the Chichester District Council, owners of Pallant House, of the Dean's collection for display at Pallant

House assured the future of this excellent example of provincial Baroque architecture.

In its restored state, Pallant House pays tribute to two men who, separated by 250 years, each contributed significantly to the artistic heritage of twentieth-century Chichester. Henry Peckham, the eighteenth-century merchant whose home has been a model to which architects have aspired both in his own time and in more recent years, would surely have admired the taste and discretion of Walter Hussey, the twentieth-century churchman and devoted patron of the arts who, during his career as vicar of St. Matthew's Church in Northampton (1937-55) and later as Dean of Chichester Cathedral (1955-77) enriched the churches under his care with the works of living artists.

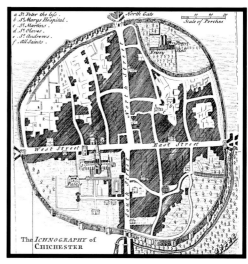

Emanuel Bowen's map of Chichester of 1749, showing The Pallant, the south-east quarter of the city, and Pallant House at its centre.

Henry Moore and Graham Sutherland received some of their first public commissions from Dr. Hussey, and remained his lifelong friends. At the Cathedral, and in St. Matthew's, we see the fruits of Hussey's work in his official capacity; at Pallant House, we are privileged to enjoy the paintings, drawings, prints and sculpture that he collected together over many years for his own pleasure.

Since 1982, when the house was first opened to the public, Pallant House has been fortunate in acquiring other works of art which complement both the Hussey Bequest and the house itself. The porcelain of the Geoffrey Freeman Collection is typical of the china that would have been in everyday use in a

Samuel & Nathaniel Buck: *The South-West Prospect of the City of Chichester* (1738). Detail, showing the roof of Pallant house, with its stairhead and balustrade

4

merchant's house in the 1750s and 1760s. The Peckhams, and their successors, whose 'modernisations' have been the basis for deciding the period style to which each room should be restored, would feel quite at home with the antique furniture, the glassware, the silhouette portraits and the Victorian kitchen. And Dean Hussey would certainly have approved of the bequest of paintings left to Pallant House in 1989 by Charles Kearley, a builder whose love of modern art was inspired by its use in modern interiors.

In addition to the permanent collections, a programme of temporary exhibitions is organised in the modern galleries at the back of the house, and the Friends of Pallant House arrange lectures, concerts and outings. Visitors may also enjoy the peace of the walled garden, designed to re-create as nearly as possible an eighteenth-century town garden, stocked only with plants that would have been available to the eighteenth-century gardener.

The restoration of the house, a co-operative project of the Chichester District Council and the Friends of Pallant House, was largely completed by August 1987, always with enormous care and attention to authentic period detail, and always with a view to the long-term conservation of this most English of English houses and the revelation of its own particular inherent characteristics.

Anon. English School: *East Street, Chichester in 1715*
The only picture that shows the ordinary street scene in the city during the eighteenth century. The round building to the left of the Market Cross is the Water Conduit House. Almost all the figures are identifiable.

5

ARCHITECTURE

Long recognised by architectural historians as one of the most important eighteenth-century town houses in England, Pallant House was originally built in 1712/13 by a young wine merchant and his wife. After almost 270 years of private ownership, its significance was finally acknowledged by the inhabitants of Chichester. Restoration began early in 1980, and the house was first opened to the public in May, 1982.

Externally, Pallant House is, to modern eyes, elegant, restrained and the epitome of Englishness. But in its time it was the height of modernism. Its style, its materials and its size would have been very new to Chichester in the early eighteenth-century. Although nothing has survived of contemporary local comment about the house, it would be safe to assume that its aggressive novelty would not have passed unnoticed.

Its Baroque features must have looked positively outlandish to the inhabitants of Chichester at the end of Queen Anne's reign. James Spershott, the eighteenth-century historian of Chichester, tells us that in his youth "the city had a very mean appearance in comparison of what it has since arrived to. The buildings were in general very low, very old, and their fronts framed with timber which lay bare to the weather, and had a step down from the street to the ground floor... There were very few houses even in the main streets that had solid brick fronts."

The immediate neighbourhood of this south-east quarter of the city was mostly made up of brewhouses, malthouses and washrooms; Pallant House was itself built on the foundations of an old malthouse, a relic of the declining brewing industry in Chichester. Any dwellings that did exist there would have been timber-framed, their jettied first floors overhanging unpaved streets down which herdsmen still drove their sheep and cattle.

The Pallant was in those days distinctly less salubrious than present appearances would suggest. This quarter of the city had for many years been the preserve of the leatherworkers and tanners; the unsavoury evidence of their notoriously malodorous craft would have been all too evident in the air of the district.

It was in the middle of this industrial quarter that the twenty-seven year old Henry Peckham and his wife Elizabeth chose to build their new home and

Facing Page: 'Swan House'. An old photograph, dating from around 1895 when the house was still privately occupied.

business in 1712. Sweeping aside the old malthouse (of which parts still survive in the present structure), and the ancient wooden market cross at the centre of the Pallant where the tanners and curriers had met and traded for centuries, the Peckhams built themselves a house that was calculated to impress and overawe, proclaiming the importance and standing of its owners to the local populace.

No architect is directly associated with the building of Pallant House. Clearly, the old attribution to Sir Christopher Wren was always optimistic, although not altogether misplaced; the overall appearance of the house, with its classically simple symmetry and carefully calculated proportions, relies heavily on the rules of that 'natural beauty' that was always his aim. Wren's only known connection with Chichester is his visit in 1684 when he was called in to advise on the rebuilding of the north-west tower of the Cathedral that had collapsed about fifty years earlier.

The design of Pallant House clearly entailed a good deal of discussion as to its style, materials and structure. At the time, it was the usual practice to select a particular model for a new house either from a pattern-book or from an existing building, and to adapt this to individual needs and requirements with the help of a competent mason or carpenter. This is exactly what the Peckhams did; using a particular style or "modell" of London house with which he was familiar as a basis, he and Elizabeth instructed the master mason, Henry Smart, to copy it in Chichester with certain improvements.

Pallant House. The street front. Henry Peckham's monogram in gilt letters can be seen between the gateposts.

London would certainly have been a useful 'sourcebook' of designs. The building trade was flourishing, and massive building schemes were changing the face of the capital. Acts of Parliament which regulated certain features of house-building were to have a far-reaching effect on design. The 1667 Act not only dictated that the size of the house should reflect the width of the street where it was built, but also that façades should be of solid brick or stone construction rather than the traditional timber-frame with wattle-and-daub. The 1707 Act prohibited the use of decorative wooden eaves cornices (which had allowed fire to spread), suggesting that the façade should instead be continued above eaves level for at least eighteen inches to form a parapet around the pitched roof. The Supplementary Act of 1709 further directed that sash windows, with their abundance of combustible timber, should be set at least four inches back from the brick face. So, although these laws were not strictly adhered to by

all builders, it should in theory be possible to date the prototype of Peckham's house between 1707 and 1709, bearing in mind that it has the new-style parapet, but that its sash windows are more or less flush with the façade, in the old manner.

The aggressively regular and symmetrical façade of the house, which echoes the arrangement of the rooms inside, has seven bays, divided vertically into three sections, the central section of these bays being set slightly forward. Horizontal articulation is supplied by a cut brick string-course at first-floor level, and a brick eaves cornice supporting the parapet. These, together with the rusticated quoins at the corners of the building, give the façade great visual strength and unity.

The main block of the house is set above street level upon a basement storey and back from the street behind a generous forecourt. The parapet almost conceals the tiled roof, but the lofty pannelled-brick chimneys add considerably to the impressiveness of this façade. The northern chimney stack, with its brick structure that allows access to the flat roof from the back stairs, is a later (but still early eighteenth-century) modification, which also appears to have included a railing around the flat roof area.

Pallant House. The street front.

The fascinating and extraordinary feature of Pallant House is its very fine detail. Normally, a house of this period will proclaim the profession of its builder; a bricklayer will show his own virtuosity and play down the role of the carpenter, glazier or blacksmith, and so on. Pallant House is blessed with outstanding craftsmanship in all the building skills. Most obvious, perhaps, is the fine brickwork, particularly in the transoms or window lintels; these are of rubbed and finely gauged brick, set in putty joints. Their flat arches have blind serpentine soffits on the face, in imitation of softly draped pelmets, and in the centre of each one is a brick "keystone", carved with an armorial device representing the royal families and realms of Great Britain. These include a rose (for England and the houses of York, Lancaster and Tudor), a thistle (for Scotland), a harp (Ireland), a fleur-de-lys (House of Plantagenet), an oak sprig (House of Stuart), a tulip (House of Orange) and another as yet unidentified. The large arched window on the rear façade is topped with a "keystone" decorated with an elaborate motif of three tulips in a pot. The structural brickwork is of Flemish bond.

Two minor details show some of the care and attention that has gone into the design. One is the difference in the inner and outer quoins. Those on the outside corners of the house are rusticated, whereas those on the angles of the projecting central section are not, giving an added visual strength to those outer corners. The other detail, even less obvious, is the increased height (of 150mm) of the upper windows over that of the lower ones. This was presumably intended to add to the impression of verticality given by the splendid façade.

In the grandiose timber doorcase, with its Corinthian pilasters and segmental-arched pediment, set in the middle of the central bay, we see the craft of the carpenter at its finest, and the exceptional wrought-iron railing around the forecourt and in the overthrow between the gate piers (with its gilded 'H.P.' monogram) shows the craftsman blacksmith at his very best. The wrought-iron gates that used to hang on the piers were removed more than eighty years ago and no record survives of their design. The glazier was certainly well represented, although the present sashes, with their narrow glazing bars are later replacements of rather heavy originals (of which the only survivor can be seen in the rear façade). Even the mason, in this almost stone-free façade, is not neglected. The two stone birds on the gate piers, proud guardians of the house for almost three centuries, are a remarkable survival of early eighteenth century provincial stone-carving. They are intended to represent ostriches, the adopted crest of the Peckham family, but their rather truncated and inelegant anatomy has led to the house's affectionate local nickname "The Dodo House", presumably not the effect desired by Peckham when he commissioned them.

One of the most fascinating things about Henry Peckham's house is that it is such an emphatic expression of one sector of English society in the early eighteenth century. 1712 saw the creation of John Bull as a cloth merchant in John Arbuthnot's pamphlet "Law is a Bottomless Pit". This epitome of Englishness would have felt very much at home here; the very siting of the house, not out in the country on an estate, but within the thriving industrial quarter of a city whose wealth depended on trade and agriculture, was significant. Peckham obviously agreed with his contemporary, Daniel Defoe, who wrote that "An estate is but a pond...but trade is a spring".

We also know that Peckham, for most of his life, was active in Tory politics, setting him against the excise duties being imposed by Walpole's Whigs, and against the war with Spain. The combination of this sympathy and the royal emblems on the façade of the house would also indicate Jacobite leanings, but this must remain supposition.

In the eventful years of the early eighteenth century, architecture played a leading and controversial role. During the Tories' brief moment of power (1710-14), when Pallant House was built, feelings of nationalistic self-confidence initiated a building boom all over the country. The English Baroque of Sir Christopher Wren was the Tories' preferred style, and it is to this style that the English merchant tended, in preference to the Whiggish Palladianism that was to dominate architectural styles in this country for the next five or six decades.

Both in its external appearance and in much of its interior detail, Pallant House is closely related to a contemporary group of houses in Kent; Westwell in Tenterden (1711), Bradbourne at East Malling (1713), Ferox Hall in Tonbridge and West Farleigh Hall (1719), each built within six years of Pallant House, all have features in common with it, particularly in their brickwork and joinery. So far, no evidence of any actual relationship between this group and Pallant House has been discovered.

"The Dodos" - Pallant House in 1939. A photograph taken by F. Goldring. The ostrich 'proper' was the adopted crest of the Peckham family. These unusual sculptures, contemporary with the house, are intended to represent ostriches, but have given the house its local nickname "The Dodo House".

INTERIOR

Despite its appearance, and in contrast with the Kent group, Pallant House is not a large house. All the design features of the façade conspire to make it appear so, and this conspiracy is even carried on into the interior. The Entrance Hall occupies the entire depth of the house and almost one-third of its width, a very prodigal use of space considering the already restricted area available for the main reception rooms, and the substantial ground sacrificed to the forecourt.

Having negotiated the ten stone steps and monstrously large front door, the visitor was shown into an entrance hall worthy of a country mansion. Whilst large, this room has little decoration; the simple panelling, the elliptical archway under the stairs and the plain stone-flagged floor all contribute to give a strong illusion of depth, and also to heighten the very decorative effect of the magnificent carved oak staircase, one of the original features of the house. Around the edges of the floor, small plugs of lead are set into the stone; these would have allowed a carpet to be laid and pinned, probably just for special occasions.

Compared with the dark, cold and airless houses of previous centuries, the age of Hogarth saw a revolution in the standards of ordinary housing that has not been equalled until the present century. Behind symmetrical classical façades, interiors became at once light, airy, clean and, above all, 'convenient', an overriding priority for houses at that time. The Entrance Hall and Dining Room at Pallant House are absolutely typical of the period, with their large windows, sparse furnishings, clean lines and austere formality; Henry Peckham would recognise these rooms and feel quite at home here.

After the grandeur of the Entrance Hall, the rooms leading from it are of more modest proportions. On the left of the main entrance is the Dining Room, with its original panelling still largely intact. By any standards this is not a large room, and it would seem more likely that it was originally intended for a business office rather than any sort of reception room. During restoration, a very tantalising fragment of newspaper was found here which includes an advertisement announcing that 'a little parcel of the best French Clarets, Obrion and Medoc, lately come from Guernsey, are to be sold by Hogsheads at 30gns, by dozens at 33s...'. This fragment is dateable between 1711 and 1717.

Henry Peckham's own dining room is likely to have been one half of the large room on the other side of the Entrance Hall, overlooking the street. In the other

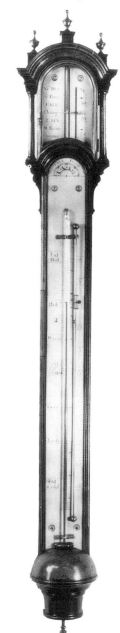

A barometer by Benjamin Cole of around 1720. The scale of the thermometer runs from 95° at "extra cold" to 0° at "extra hot", a predecessor of Fahrenheit and Centigrade called the Royal Society Scale. For obvious reasons, this was soon phased out.

The Entrance Hall.

half, the 'drawing room' would have overlooked the garden. Originally, the alcoves either side of the fireplaces in these two rooms contained windows, probably blocked in when the houses opposite became private dwellings.

Beneath this floor lies the barrel-vaulted basement, with its flint-lined cess-pit, its well, and seven smaller rooms clustered around the large central area. The stone-lined well and much of the brickwork at this level appear to pre-date Pallant House. Here were the fuel stores, the beer and wine cellars for the house and, no doubt, Henry Peckham's stock-in-trade of Portugal wines.

Leaving the formal reception areas on the ground floor, the Peckham's friends and relatives would have been received and entertained, on less formal occasions, on the first floor. The central room, Mrs. Peckham's 'Parlour Chamber' or Ante-Room, is given more importance than any other room in the house by its design features; it has three windows overlooking the street front; it has heavy, raised-and-fielded panelling and it has the large arched doorway opening onto the landing of the main staircase, echoing the shape of the window lighting that staircase. In here, the Peckhams would have shown off their best furniture, hung their ancestral portraits and entertained their guests to tea.

Leading off the Parlour Chamber are two other rooms, one of which (to the south) must have been a bedroom; the other, which has no space for a bed, appears to have been a family sitting-room. Easily reached by the servants from the adjacent back stairs, and provided as it is with the conveniences of a closet (with privy shaft running down to the cess-pit in the basement), a wardrobe cupboard (complete with some of its original hanging-pegs) and a coal cupboard concealed in the panelling, this room, with its magnificent views across the rooftops of Chichester to the Cathedral, gives all the appearances of having been well used and well loved.

The Bedroom, on the other side of the Parlour Chamber, was originally plastered and decorated with wallpaper. The present panelling dates from around 1780. There was at one time a large opening, possibly with double doors, through the wall to the adjacent room, which may originally have been Mrs. Peckham's dressing room, but is now restored as a nineteenth century collector's room or 'Cabinet'. As in the room below, the Bedroom and Cabinet also originally had windows either side of the fireplaces. In the Bedroom, the two embrasures were turned into closets when the panelling was installed. The Cabinet was

Facing page: The Hall as it was around 1915. The pictures on the walls are reproductions of the Raphael cartoons at the Victoria and Albert Museum. The wall over the panelling and the fields of the panels are decorated with wallpaper.

A detail of the Hall, showing an example of the old 'strap' hinge, and three of the lead plugs, let into the edge of the stone floor to allow a carpet to be pinned.

one of the rooms modernised probably in the 1830s, by Joseph Godman, a gentleman farmer who lived at Pallant House from 1796 until 1840. Its restoration as a 'Cabinet' is entirely in keeping with fashions of this period, and allows the display of watercolours, drawings and prints from the fine art collections belonging to Pallant House.

The fifth room on this floor, adjoining the back stairs and overlooking the garden, has suffered more than any other from the depredations of time and successive owners; what panelling remains is incomplete, some possibly even second-hand, and badly damaged; the original window shutters have been removed; and from the evidence of the two different cornices, it looks as though a partition wall has been demolished. We know from some plans of 1902/3 that the end nearest the front staircase was a bathroom at that time. It can be assumed from the position of the room itself that it was the room of a housekeeper or senior servant.

Immediately below this room is the Victorian Kitchen. We know that Mrs. Peckham's objection to the proposed basement kitchen led to the building of an extension at the back of the house, and old maps of the town show the rough shape of this. The room now restored as a kitchen would have been the Servants' Hall and pantry, where the dishes of food coming from the kitchen beyond would have been properly dressed and garnished for Mrs. Peckham's dining table.The present extension at the back of the house dates from around 1800, and appears on a map of 1812. From evidence in the deeds of Pallant House, it appears that this was originally built as an extension to the house next door, then owned by John Marsh, the composer, only being transferred to the ownership of Joseph Godman in 1833.

Godman's household included two manservants and four serving women, all of whom would presumably have been lodged in the six attic rooms of the second floor.

When the house was sold in 1896 after the death of William Duke, a solicitor who had owned it since 1851, it is described as having a 'lofty Entrance Hall', a library (now the Dining Room), a pantry, scullery, kitchen and W.C. with two rooms beyond. On the first floor, five bedrooms and a W.C. are mentioned, with a further four on the second floor, there was a 'good Garden', a conservatory and closet, as well as a stable-yard, a two-stalled stable and harness room with a loft over, and a chaise-house. Most of the 'good Garden' has now disappeared, largely because of the addition of the large room to the rear of the house, built by the then owners, the Rural District Council, as a Council Chamber, but the stable and chaise-house survive further along East Pallant, now adapted as private dwellings.

A detail of the original carved oak staircase, with two of the carved 'strings', the lower one depicting two crossed clay pipes, billowing smoke.

Right: The fireplace in the Dining Room. The original surround of flat marble 'tables' and without mantelpiece is typical of the period, as is the overmantel looking-glass with candle sconces.

Below: A detail of the marble fireplace that was removed in the 1970s. This had probably been installed in the Entrance Hall in the late eighteenth century.

RECENT HISTORY

Although it may have protected the house from the ravages of the interior decorator, the sixty years of local government occupation (1919-79) cannot be said to have been of any great benefit to the house. Old fixtures and fittings were stripped out, partitions were erected in the rooms, and the essential character of the house, built up over two hundred years of private occupation, disappeared. The 1934 extension, with its 1960s addition opposite the back door of the house effectively destroyed not only the outlook from this side of the house, but also the proper appreciation of its rear elevation.

However, with the Chichester District Council's decision, in 1979, to accept the offer of Dean Hussey to give his fine art collection to Chichester for display at Pallant House, the process of decay was finally reversed, and a comprehensive programme of restoration and redecoration was initiated as a joint venture by the District Council and the newly formed Friends of Pallant House. The aim of this joint scheme was to provide a sympathetic setting for Dean Hussey's collection, and to restore the interior of the house, as far as possible, to what it had been at certain given periods of its two hundred and seventy year history, all executed to the highest standards of historical accuracy, particularly where the paint finishes and colours are concerned. The result is a combination of period house and art gallery, in which a Henry Moore drawing can hang happily over an exquisite ladies' writing desk of about 1780, in which eighteenth century paintings, furniture, porcelain and glass can be seen against authentic period-style backgrounds which make us question accepted ideas of historic interior decoration, and in which we may easily visualise an imaginative and sensitive modern-day collector living and displaying his treasures.

DAVID COKE

NOTE
Most documentation for this text is drawn from the 'Pallant House' Deeds (1795 to date) in the hands of the Chichester District Council, as well as from two 'sale' advertisements (1782 and 1896).

BIBLIOGRAPHY
NATHANIEL LLOYD: *Gems of English Architecture IV Wren's House and Pallant House Chichester.* In 'Architectural Review' May 1919 pp 89-92
DAVID COKE: *Pallant House, Chichester.* Part I & II in 'West Sussex History' Nos. 23 & 24, Sept. 1982 & Jan. 1983
ANON: *Wren's House and Pallant House, Chichester.* In 'Country Life' April 27 1912 pp 614-619

Looking from the first floor landing into the 'Cabinet', Bedroom and Ante-Room.

A Regulator Clock by Edward Box of Chichester (around 1800) with a detail of the movement and winding gear.

Henry Peckham of Pallant House

ANCESTRY AND EARLY LIFE

Henry Peckham of Pallant House was baptised on 12 July 1683 at the church of St Peter the Less, North Street, Chichester. His father, Captain John Peckham, a disreputable figure who briefly held a commission in the Army, was living at the time at Boxgrove where the Peckham family had been established for at least five generations.[1] Their earliest recorded ancestor, Edward Peckham, is traceable at Boxgrove from 1571. This Edward Peckham prospered, married well and in 1584 joined the ranks of the West Sussex gentry when he bought from Lord Lumley the manor of Easthampnett in Boxgrove. Edward Peckham's eldest son, Henry Peckham (c. 1570-1616), the first member of the family to be educated at Oxford, served as coroner for the western division of Sussex from 1603 until his death.[2] In later generations many of the Peckhams' sons were drawn into the mercantile or professional worlds of Chichester, while others farmed at Boxgrove or Aldingbourne; another branch settled at Compton and thereabouts.

The most distinguished member of the family was Sir Henry Peckham (1614-73), a grandson of the coroner and himself grandfather of Henry Peckham of Pallant House.[3] Throughout his long legal and political career, Sir Henry maintained strong links with the city of Chichester. After Magdalen, Oxford, he progressed to the Middle Temple, his professional life as a lawyer beginning just as the Civil War drew to a close, and continuing with few checks throughout the subsequent political upheavals. Although clearly a court supporter, his views were moderate, and he successfully held office under the Protectorate. In 1654 he became Recorder of Chichester and was elected a member of Parliament for the city, being returned on four subsequent occasions; he was still in possession of the seat at his death nearly twenty years later. Sir Henry received a knighthood in 1662, and in 1669 took the degree of serjeant-at-law; John Evelyn attended his reading feast and describes the occasion in his diary. Marriage with Judith Goring in 1644 brought Sir Henry many powerful connections in West Sussex and beyond. When he died in 1673 he had a well-appointed house in West Street, Chichester, a country house at Crockerhill, Boxgrove, and chambers in the Middle Temple which reflected his status as serjeant-at-law.

A corner of the Study, looking out over the rooftops of Chichester towards the Cathedral.

Sir Henry admitted in his will that 'it hath pleased my good God to blesse me with all farr beyond my Expectations and deserveings', and he left considerable property in Sussex.[4] But at his death his affairs were in disorder and his estate took some years to settle.

When Sir Henry Peckham drew up his will shortly before he died, he evidently recognised that the interests of his third son, John, ranged beyond the trades and professions of Chichester. He explains that he had discussed the boy's future with three directors of the East India Company, Lord Berkeley, Sir John Robinson and Nathaniel Herne, the deputy-governor, all of whom had offered their patronage, and that should John decide to go to the East Indies money should be made available for him to do so. It is not known whether John Peckham ventured abroad at this stage of his life, but in May 1678, five years after his father's death, he was commissioned at Whitehall as a captain in Sir Thomas Slingsby's regiment which served that year in Flanders.[5] The captain of John's troop was a Sussex baronet, Sir James Bowyer of Leythorne, near Chichester, which would explain his choice of regiment.

In 1682 John Peckham married Joan Young, a widow in comfortable circumstances. She was the daughter of a rich farmer, Gregory Hurst of Toat, near Pulborough; there is evidence in a Chancery suit to suggest that Hurst was unhappy at her choice.[6] Joan's first husband, Thomas Young, farmed some 220 acres at South Mundham until his death in 1679. Young's parents made over to him when he was a child in 1647 a sixth part of South Mundham Farm, and later he was able to buy out the co-owners, completing the purchase in 1671, about the time of his marriage to Joan.[7] The present house of two storeys and seven window bays has an elegant gabled façade with a much older building behind. This façade is in the Artisan Mannerist style and bears the date 1671, so it seems likely that Young and his wife were responsible for this embellishment. They had one daughter named Anne who married William Peachey.

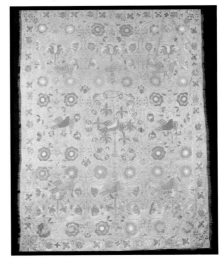

Indo-Portuguese silk bedcover with couched embroidery.

John and Joan Peckham began their married life at Crockerhill, Boxgrove. In 1690 they moved to the farm at South Mundham where their five surviving children - two boys and three girls - were brought up. The possession of the farm (which had been settled upon Joan at the time of her first marriage) provided a lifeline as John's affairs became more chaotic. He and his equally disreputable brother, William, frittered away or encumbered the remainder of their grandfather's estate, and they were not helped by the indolent executors. John had inherited from his father the reversion of the Nyton estate at Aldingbourne which he sold, already mortgaged, to his cousin Thomas Peckham, an Arundel attorney. Thomas, who had come to John's rescue with money when he was sick and destitute in London, discovered half way through the transaction that John had no right to sell as his father's estate had not been settled. The Chancery suit Thomas was forced to bring throws poor light on John's character.[8] Later John attempted to defraud his own son Henry of the lease of Norton's Farm at Aldingbourne which was left to the infant in 1687 by his uncle, Robert Peckham of Chichester. Fortunately one of the executors, Thomas Carr, took immediate action when he heard that John was attempting to upset the will, with the result that it was not proved until Henry was of age.[9]

After John's death in 1700 Joan turned to a Chichester attorney, James Vavasor, who offered to help disentangle the muddle John left behind. At some point John had insisted on mortgaging the farm, and complications over this debt almost led to the family's eviction. Vavasor explained in a statement to the Chancery court that the Peckhams 'had not the most provident way of managing their estate & affaires' which was evidently a fair comment, and that John died 'in a very poore & meane condicion & his widow…[was] left very destitute & helpless'. John died intestate; he had in his possession at the time of his death 'a Mace, a pair of Pistoles, a Gun, Some Arrears of Rent…some household Goods of inconsid[er]able Value & the Corn & Grain Sown or growing on the Mortgaged prem[ise]s'.[10] It is recorded that Vavasor gave the gun to Henry. A tenant was found to work the land and Joan was paid £60 a year to manage the farm and pay off the debts. With family life at South Mundham Farm severely restricted by poverty, the wider horizons which Sir Henry's career and marriage had opened up to his family were closed. Joan had no members of her own family to turn to: she was at loggerheads with her nearest relation, her half-sister Katherine Penford, whom she accused of appropriating the entire estate of their father Gregory Hurst.[11] Thus family responsibilities fell heavily on Henry, the eldest child, who was sixteen at the time of his father's death. Although the evidence makes clear that Henry's circumstances were better than those of his mother or his siblings, it is possible that the humiliations of these years of privation left their mark upon his personality. Thomas Carr, his guardian, allowed him money to buy clothes and other necessary items, and Vavasor, recognising that the boy had promise and was wasting his time doing

One of the original door locks to have survived, this one is on the inside of the door to the lavatory-cupboard adjoining the Study.

menial tasks about the farm, took him into his house in Chichester. Vavasor (elected Mayor of the city in 1707), described himself as a close friend of Henry's father and was married to Anne Ludgater, a kinswoman of Joan. He intended to start Henry off on an attorney's career, but in this he was disappointed because after nine months in Vavasor's office doing 'what business in writing [Vavasor] sett him about', Henry left. According to Vavasor, Henry's 'impudent behavious & inclinacon to be a soldier caused him to depart...& go into the Army.'[12] Nothing further is known of this period of Henry's life, and his name does not occur in the list of commissioned officers.

By 1711 John Peckham's debts had been paid off. Henry and his mother successfully applied to the court for the restitution of their rights, and Henry took over the running of South Mundham Farm. It was rumoured in Chichester that Henry lost money during the three years that he tried to make improvements to the property, but by the end of that time his circumstances changed so completely that he could safely ignore any deficit.[13]

Facing page : South Mundham House (a few miles south of Chichester) as it appears today. The date 1671 and initials 'T.Y.' for Thomas Young appear in the segmental pediment over the front door. Henry Peckham lived here with his family from 1690 until after 1700.   PHOTO: CLAIRE LAKE

HENRY PECKHAM'S MARRIAGE

On 20 May 1711 Henry Peckham married Elizabeth Albery at the church of St Martin Outwich in the City of London. He was twenty-seven and his bride a widow in her early forties. It is likely that they met in Sussex because Elizabeth's first husband, the Revd John Albery, was vicar between 1703 and 1706 of Hunston, a farming hamlet a mile from South Mundham. Elizabeth herself was brought up at Ferring where her father, the Revd Charles Cutter, was vicar from 1670 until his death in 1716. Cutter who was described by his Bishop as 'a generous, stout, welbred gentleman, a true sonn of the Ch: of England', was formerly curate at Albury, near Guildford, where four of his children (but not Elizabeth) were baptised between 1664 and 1667.[14] His wife, Susan, died in childbirth soon after their arrival at Ferring; Cutter remarried, but his second wife died, apparently childless, in 1686.[15] Elizabeth was undoubtedly a child of the first marriage, and there are reasons to believe that she was the youngest, thus placing her birth in 1668 or 1669.[16] Only one other Cutter child, Vincent, survived infancy. He joined the Royal Navy, so their widowed father's dependence on Elizabeth may account for the lateness - by contemporary standards - of her first marriage, which took place at Ferring in 1698 when she was about thirty. John Albery, her husband, came from a well-known Arundel family and was at the time of his marriage vicar of Tortington, a mile or so to the south. He was also curate of Houghton where he and Elizabeth lived and where their only child, John, was baptised on 27 September 1700. Young John survived for only seven months and was buried at Arundel.[17] In 1706 Albery himself died. Elizabeth's devotion to the memory of her first husband (and their child) is evident from the directions she left in her will over forty years later: 'I desire my Body may be carried in a Hearse to Arundell and buryed there by my late husband Albery as privately as conveniently may be'.[18]

In 1710 Elizabeth's brother Vincent died having accumulated a large fortune. Vincent Cutter was a childless widower, and he made his sister his principal beneficiary. Cutter had risen to the rank of captain in the Royal Navy and at the time of his death Elizabeth discovered that there was money due to his estate for pay and allowances as well as prize money.[19] Cutter's fortune was largely based on the mercantile activities in which naval officers were at that time allowed to participate; he had holdings of government and East India Company stock, also the lease of a grand London house - 10 Soho Square (in the north-

Facing page: A pharmacist's account addressed to "Mr. Hen. Peckham, in ye Pallant" and dated June 1730. The date of the first entry is 8th August 1713. The most expensive item is "The Cure of the Boys Leg" on April 15th 1717, at a cost of ten shillings.

west corner and still extant) - which was let to the Treasurer of the Navy, Sir Thomas Littleton. Thus the young widow found herself in possession of about £10,000 at a time when an income of £50 a year enabled a family to live well and to keep a servant. Almost exactly twelve months after Cutter's will was proved Elizabeth remarried. A happy marriage would have run its course in peaceful anonymity; but Elizabeth's marriage to Henry Peckham failed, and the circumstances of its failure were examined by the Court of Chancery. The proceedings were carefully transcribed at the time by clerks and, as neither of the litigants was prepared to settle, the suit dragged on for some years. For this reason the records are extensive, and the details which emerge include valuable information about the building of Pallant House.[20]

Elizabeth's evidence describes how in April 1711 Henry 'made application...with pretensions of great love & kindness & many fair promises in order to marriage'; proposals about a settlement were put forward by Elizabeth at the insistence of her father, and one of these proposals was found 'to be soe unreasonable' by Henry, that, for a time, he 'did actually discontinue his addresses...on that very account'. Elizabeth's demands do not sound excessive today, particularly as the money concerned was all her own. Henry agreed to her request for £50 pin money each year to spend as she pleased, but found quite unacceptable her desire to leave £2,000 in her will to whom she chose. Almost equally unpalatable was her wish to be left £5,000 by him should he die before her. Henry realised that a large capital sum would be tied up, but under duress he agreed to make these provisions and also to render accounts of the investments from time to time. Henry explains in his evidence that it was necessary to placate his future father-in-law, Elizabeth 'having some expectations from him'. Probably he was also taking account of Cutter's temper which had already landed the vicar in trouble for 'contumelious' language against a chimney tax collector.[21] Henry was quite candid about the expectations he had of their marriage, having heard, he states, from several of Elizabeth's friends and acquaintances that she was worth 'at least £10,000', while Elizabeth herself by 'frequent declarations & insinuations' implied 'she was worth about £7,000'. Thus, on 20 May, six days after the signing of the marriage settlement, Henry married, thereby acquiring a fortune and a wife who, though naive, knew her own mind. Elizabeth, emerging from her sheltered background of Sussex vicarages, can have had no conception of the worldly ways of her ambitious young second husband. What little we know of her first, John Albery, whose immediate forbears at Arundel had suffered for their Puritan sympathies, does not suggest any particular attachment to Mammon. It is hardly surprising that Elizabeth was cautious, but there is evidence to suggest that she was also 'close' in her financial dealings. There is little doubt that she acted unfairly when she allowed a dispute with her brother's agent to reach the Court of Chancery, and her will reveals that she considered *twenty-eight* an appropriate age for a beneficiary to inherit.[22] And yet Elizabeth frankly admitted her role in the principal extravagance of the marriage: the building of Pallant House.

The signatures of Henry and Elizabeth Peckham from one of the Chancery Documents at the Public Record Office.

THE BUILDING OF PALLANT HOUSE

In her evidence Elizabeth did not contest Henry's claim that she made the original suggestion to build a house in Chichester, that she made alterations as the building progressed whether Henry was present or not, and that she pressed him to dig into her fortune as necessary to pay the bills. On this subject Henry's answer states:

> ye same became much more expensive & cost much more money than this Def[endant] at first proposed or intended to have laid out...he verily believes that the building & ffinishing thereof...did not cost... less than Three Thousand pounds or thereabouts.

The question of how much money was spent by the Peckhams on Pallant House soon became the main issue, and to establish this eight craftsmen who worked on the building were summoned by the court to attend on 14 October 1717 at the Black Horse in Chichester. The sworn statements of these men - James Burley (joiner), John Channell (carpenter), Richard Clayton (carpenter), Edward Lawrence (bricklayer), Richard Moorey (bricklayer), John Page (carpenter), John Pryor (joiner) and Henry Smart (mason) - provide the only information found up to the present time about the construction of Pallant House.[23] From this testimony we learn that Henry Smart, a Chichester mason, provided at the Peckham's request 'a fframe or Modell' for a house; and that later the Peckhams left for London and returned with another design. Smart is quite specific, describing it as 'a New Modell...Drawne at London', and John Channell confirms this, referring in his evidence to 'the Draught or Modell of the Dwellinghouse & Outhouses...brought from London'. We know that this second design was made to Henry's specification because when he, on his return from London, presents it to Smart, he asks Smart 'to explaine the said Modell' to Elizabeth, and she at once objected to the position of the kitchen in the basement, insisting that it would be 'too cold & damp for herselfe & servants'. After examining the new plan, Smart estimated that it would cost at least £1,600 to build, making clear that the figure for his own would be less. Financial considerations did not appear to affect Elizabeth's enthusiasm and, adds Smart, 'upon her liking it...Peckham proceeded & built the said House according to the London Modell'.

The statements given to the court show that Henry consulted Elizabeth

Supplement to Catalogue.

(new acquisitions since 1990: date of current published catalogue).

CHCPH No.	Artist & Works held.	Details.
A		
	ANON (19th C British:Wm.Inkson?):	
667	*39 Chichester Characters*(c.1850s):	DW:131x60(x39):Pr VMeynell 1993.
B		
	BAIER, Fred (b.1949):	
817	*Mirror in Square & Elliptical frame* (1993):	Rw:610x880x45:Pr DEdwards 1993.
	BARKER, Kit (1916-1988)	
882	*Gathered Reeds, Grande-Briere* (d.1969)	Oc:500x960:X:Pr Mrs Barker 1995
891	*Llanmadoc, Gower* (1965)	Oc:510x863:X:Bq MrsDMLucas 1995
	BELLEROCHE, Willie de (b.1920)	
626	*Ferelyth* (d.1938)	D:228x280 Bq Kearley 1989
	BONE, Sir Muirhead (1876-1953)	
712	*East Street, Chichester* (d.1907)	D:115x160:X: Bt Phillips(FPH) 1992
	BRADEN, Norah (b.1901)	
827	*Unglazed Handled Jug*	Y:230x105 Bt FPH 1994
897	*Jar with brown brush stroke decoration*	Y:243x223 Bq MrsDMLucas 1995
	BREWSTER, Martyn (b.1952)	
840	*Garden Series No.1* (1993)	I:195x145 Pr the artist 1995
	BROWN, Percy, (b.1911)	
642	*Untitled piece* (Aluminium)	Sm:320x290x100 Pr the artist 1990
703	*Stoneware Vase* (1991)	Y:322x140x85 Pr the artist 1992

C

CARDEW, Michael (1901-1993)

896	*Brown Jug with Handle*	Y:214x193 Bq MrsDMLucas 1995

CASSON, Sir Hugh (b.1910)

633	*John Keats House, Chichester* (1975)	D:135x170 Pr N.Colyer 1990

CATT, George Herbert (1869-1920)

835	Sketchbook of Fabric Designs	D:128x178:Pr BCatt 1994
836	Sketchbook of Architectural devices	D:128x178:Pr BCatt 1994
837	Book of Architectural Notes	D:226x183:Pr BCatt 1994
842	*Field of Corn Stooks*	W:230x353;Pr BCatt 1995
843	*Early Summer Downland Scene*	W:260x360:Pr BCatt 1995
844	*Basket of Eggs with Flagon and Bowl*	W:398x485:Pr BCatt 1995
845	*Corn Stooks at Sunset*	W:260x366:Pr BCatt 1995
846	*Corn stooks on a hot Summer's day*	W:236x340:Pr BCatt 1995
847	*Grey dish with handles*	W:136x240:Pr BCatt 1995
848	*Beechwood in early Summer*	W:353x234:Pr BCatt 1995
849	*East Row, Chichester*	W:374x268:Pr BCatt 1995
850	(Student of) *17th C Persian Bowl*	W:340x240:Pr BCatt 1995
851	(Student of) *Design for a Sgraffito Dish*	W:757x549:Pr BCatt 1995
852	*Design for a Dado in the Persian Style*	W:565x408:Pr BCatt 1995
853	*Studies of Relief in the Gothic Style*	W:735x545:Pr BCatt 1995
854	*Studies of Surface Ornament - Gothic Style*	W:757x545:Pr BCatt 1995
855	*Designs Using Hydrangea Flower*	W:760x559:Pr BCatt 1995
856	*Designs Using Buttercup*	W:800x542:Pr BCatt 1995
857	*Ancient Orders of Architecture*	W:801x540:Pr BCatt 1995
858	*Wallflower*	W:220x127:Pr BCatt 1995
859	*View of Chilgrove*	W:165x243:Pr BCatt 1995
860	*Poppy* (1886)	W:177x125:Pr BCatt 1995
861	*View of House through alleyway*	W:245x165:Pr BCatt 1995
862	*Down a Lane, Looking out to Sea*	W:297x229:Pr BCatt 1995
863	*Orchard in Winter*	W:298x229:Pr BCatt 1995
864	*West Pallant, Chichester*	D:270x226:Pr BCatt 1995

865	*Looking down from the Downs*	W:242x348:Pr BCatt 1995
866	*Yew Tree, Kingley Vale*	W:393x278:Pr BCatt 1995
867	*View of West Pallant*	DWb:463x290:Pr BCatt 1995
868	*Cottage viewed from corn field*	W:165x244:Pr BCatt 1995

CHARLES, Bernard (b.1930   )

829	*Rotund Pot with elliptical rim*	Y:263x107x135Bt B.Charles (FPH) 1994
833	*Small Round Pot*	Y:78x41x77 Pr the artist 1994
834	*Small open dish*	Y:69x45x156 Pr the artist 1994

CLARK, Michael (b.1954   )

| 826 | *Portrait of Philip Stroud* (1993-4) | D:355x330 Pr FPH 1994 |

D

DAVIES Allan

| 687 | *Chichester Cathedral* (d.1989) | I:72x48 Pr the artist 1991 |

DUFY, Jean (1888-1964)

| 888 | *Le Cirque* | W:430x555:X:Bq MrsDMLucas 1995 |

F

FEDDEN, Mary (b.1915   )

| 691 | *The Yellow Truck* (d.1960) | Ob:500x300:X:Pr Estate of Lady C.Bonham-Carter(NACF) 1991 |

FEIBUSCH, Hans (b.1898   )

| 735 | *The Baptism of Christ* (d.1951) | G:480x220 Pr the artist 1992 |

FORSTER, Noel A.

| 636 | *Head* | L:480x320 Bq Kearley 1990 |

G

GORE, Frederick (b.1913)
House in a Winter Landscape(1932)   W:240x264:X:Bq CAEland 1995.

H

889	HALL, Patrick (1906-) *Window at Rouen II*	W:540x417:X: Bq MrsDMLucas 1995
895	HAMADA (1894-1978) *Chinese Character Motif Dish*	Y:54x330x192 Bq MrsDMLucas 1995
831	HAMILTON, Gawen (c.1697-1737) *The Rawson Conversation Piece*	Oc:800x746 Bt.Leger (NACF/VAMPGF/Sub)1994
672	HAMMOND, Henry (1914-1990) *Grass Pot*	Y:78x106x90 Pr Estate of the artist 1990
702	HAILE, Thomas Samuel 'Sam' (1909-48) *Stoneware Jug* (c.1930s)	Y:178x106x90 Pr. P.Brown 1992
822	HIRST, Derek (b.1930) *For Hokusai No.II* (1985/87)	DW:553x755:X: Pr Elephant Trust1993
883	HITCHENS, Ivon (1893-1979) *House Among Trees*	Oc:455x506:X:Bq MrsDMLucas 1995
884	*Untitled Screenprint* (1976)	L:370x506:X:Bq MrsDMLucas 1995
885	HODGKINS, Frances (1869-1947) *Dolomite Landscape*	DW:454x525:Bq MrsDMLucas1995

762	HOUTHUESEN, Albert (1903-79) *White Faced Clown*	I:590x455 Bq B.Winch 1993
662	HUDSON, Andrew (b.1953) *Nicola twice among leaves with Cameo of* *Blaine's Mushroom painting*	DW:520x740 Pr the artist 1990
671	HURRY, Leslie (1909-78) *Costume design 'The Fool' (from King Lear)*	DW:555x425:X: Pr Nicholas Byron-Irving 1990

I

814	IDEN Pottery *Brown and White Jug* (c.1950s)	Y:164x85 Bq B.Winch 1993

J

841	JOHN, Augustus (1878-1961) *Double Self-Portrait*	L:360x410:X:Pr M.Whitehorn 1995
787	JONES, David (1895-1974) *Ditchling Nativity* (1923)	Sw:1255x2130x490 Pr N.Wickham-Irving 1993

K

670	KNIGHT, Dame Laura (1877-1970) *Girl (Ballerina?) dressing her hair*	I:297x193 Pr Estate of Lady C.Bonham- Carter 1990

L

887	LAMB, Henry RA(1883-1960) *Plums on a Dish* (1939)	Oc:410x510:X:Bq MrsDMLucas 1995

	LEACH, Bernard (1887-1979)	
894i	*Red Dish*	Y:90x332x172 Bq MrsDMLucas
894ii	*Black Dish*	Y:76x370x210 Bq MrsDMLucas
894iii	*Brown Willow Tree Jar*	Y:185x225 Bq MrsDMLucas 1995

M

	MINTON, John (1917-57)	
823	*Portrait of David Tindle*	D:385x280 Bt (NADFAS) 1994

	MILLER, Geoffrey (b.1904)	
763	*Reigate Grammar School* (d.1961)	J:405x565 Bq B.Winch 1993

	MILNE, John (b.1931)	
899	*Poseidon* (1970)	Sm:605x125x120 Bq MrsDMLucas

	MITCHELL, Denis (1912-1993)	
898	*Landscape Form No.3* (1961)	Sz:200x480x133 Bq MrsDMLucas

	MOORE, Henry with BURTON, Jocelyn, silversmith	
713	*Details from 'Raising of Lazarus'* (1975) (x3)	Rm:75(d) x20(h) Bq Hussey
714	*Details from 'Raising of Lazarus'* (x3)	Rz:70(d) x23(h) Bq Hussey

	MUSZYNSKI, Leszek (b.1923)	
873	*Antonio (from Ibiza)* (1975)	P:370x290 Pr the artist 1990

N

	NASH, John, (1895-1977)	
789	*Scarborough Lily (Vallota purpurea)*	W:440x320 Pr N.Wickham-Irving 1993
886	*Landscape('boggy purple patches')*	DW:454x525 Bq MrsDMLucas 1995
	NASH, Paul (1889-1946)	
890	*For 'Urne Buriale'* (3 lithographs)	3L:245x180 Bq MrsDMLucas 1995

P

PETHER, William (1731-c.1795)
825   *Portrait of the Smith Brothers*   I:520x410 Pr MrsSRoth 1994

PIPER, John (1903-1992)
759   *Near Newcastle Emlyn, Cardigan* (1968)   I:435x635 Bq B.Winch 1993
760   *Dorchester Abbey, Oxon.* (post 1986?)   I:565x770 Bq B.Winch 1993
761   *Little Cressingham* (1983)   I:450x615 Bq B.Winch 1993
879   Fulham Pottery Mug, *Venetian Townscape*   Y:150x107:X:Bt FPH 1995
880   ditto, *Fulham Pots 1671*   Y:150x107:X:Bt FPH 1995
881   ditto, *Fulham Pottery estd 1671*   Y:150x107:X:Bt FPH 1995

PITCHFORTH, Vivian (1895-1982)
748-752   *Five sheets of Figure study sketches* (1935/6)   D:445x285 Pr Miss Cruikshank 1993

PLEYDELL-BOUVERIE, Katherine (1895-1985)
700   *Small open fluted dish*   Y:111x30x75 Pr P.Brown 1992

R

REINGANUM, Victor (1907-1995)
893   *Children Skipping*   Gob:225x305 Bq MrsDMLucas 1995

RICHARDS, Ceri (1903-71)
721   *The Rape of the Sabines* (d.1949)   W:380x555 Bt Marlborough (FPH & NACF) 1992
874   *Blossom* (1965)   CL:583x351:X:Pr A.Hewat 1994
917   *Flower* (1965)   CL:575x806:X:Pr A.Hewat 1996.

S

SEIDLER, Doris (b.1912   )
669   *The City III*   (1952)   I:428x351 Pr the artist 1990

	SHARP, Astri (b.1940)	
919	*Prebendal School Sketchbook* (1993-4)	D:296x420x15:Bt FPH 1996/ Miss Tuer Bq.
	SMITH, William (c.1707-1764)	
915	*Portrait, Charles Duke of Richmond (1701-50)*	I:345x245 Pr MrsSRoth 1995
	STENNING,P.	
723	*Pallant House*	J:103x128:X:Pr Mrs A.Clutterbuck 1992
	SYKES, Steven (b.1914)	
914	*Wittenham Clumps* (1945)	DW:325x400 Bt S.Sykes (Sub)1995
T		
	THORPE, John	
900	*Birds at Play*	Sw:370x110x80 Bq MrsDMLucas 1995
W		
	WADSWORTH, Philip Smeale (1910-1991)	
701	*Small open bowl*	Y:74x106 Pr P.Brown 1992
	WEBB, Marjorie (1903-78)	
710	*Sutherland Sunset*	Ob:515x610 Pr N.Webb 1992
	WHITE, Ethelbert (1891-1972)	
788	*Wooded Landscape*	W:455x320 Pr N.Wickham-Irving 1993
739	*Where the Hills Began*	J:86x112 Bt G.Gurrin(FPH)1992
740	*Threshing*	J:120x180 Bt G.Gurrin (FPH) 1992
	WILLIAMS, Nick	
666	*Interior, Pallant House*	W:420x300 Bt N.Williams (FPH) 1990

WILLS (nee Howard), Ferelyth
625   *Fox*   Sw:1070x225 Bq Kearley 1989

WINCH, Irene (d.1983)
815   *Buff & Red Glazed Bowl*   Y:54x160 Pr B.Winch 1993
816   *Blue-Green Glazed Bowl*   Y:53x152 Pr B.Winch 1993

{Up to 10 Jan.1996.}

throughout the construction of Pallant House, and that generally he allowed Elizabeth's taste to prevail over his. 'Where she disliked anything she had it altered', Channell comments. Several of the men refer to her interest in their work, and to the fact that she never found fault with this on her frequent inspections. When the time came to build the steps in front of the house, Henry would not allow the men to begin until Elizabeth had given her approval. Before 'the Drawing Roome Chamber' was panelled, James Bayley relates how Henry asked Elizabeth for her ideas on the subject

> And thereupon she went up Stairs into her Dressing roome with the said Deft. [Henry] & desired that the said drawing roome might be wainscotted like her dressingroom & it was done accordingly.

Some decisions Elizabeth made in Henry's absence. When John Pryor was engaged in panelling 'the parlour chamber', Elizabeth evidently decided that the result would be unsatisfactory, and, 'to make the Chamber more private', she ordered him to add a partition with a door in the middle. This must refer to the screen - still in place today on the main landing of the first floor - with its central doorway in an arched surround, flanked by Corinthian pilasters. Elizabeth's addition creates a parlour of intimate size, with good light and a view, out of what would otherwise be a draughty landing. She also directed that a window on the rear elevation of the house be removed and replaced by a much larger one, and she made unspecified alterations to a staircase.

A corner of the Kitchen, showing the only surviving original window.

The kitchen and outbuildings including the washhouse and a well-equipped brewhouse were arranged as a rear extension; 'a pair of folding doors' separated these domestic quarters from the main house. Elizabeth had an area of the cellar partitioned off to create a larder, but all the remaining space was left as cellarage. The kitchen quarters as originally built were a failure, so much so that in May 1716 the men were recalled. Richard Clayton describes how on this occasion Henry said in Elizabeth's presence 'that he had built the same to please her & it should be pulled downe & rebuilt to please her' requesting Clayton to follow Elizabeth's instructions as he was going to London '& would not medle with it having had Trouble enough about it already.' The kitchen quarters and outbuildings were duly demolished and rebuilt. Thus apart from Henry's understandable exasperation over the kitchen, the building of the house was apparently completed in harmony. Smart says that Elizabeth 'did mightily approve of the Worke'. Most of the men including Smart agreed that the final cost had been in the region of £3,000, three suggesting £2,500; Clayton estimated that the demolition and rebuilding of the kitchen quarters had been about £60.

It is not known how soon after the marriage in May 1711 the construction of Pallant House began, but the evidence suggests that once mooted by Elizabeth the project was quickly put in hand. Alexander Hay states in his history of Chichester published in 1804 that Henry Peckham built the house 'about the year 1712'. In March 1714 the Chichester Corporation gave Henry permission to demolish the wooden market cross of the leathersellers which had stood 'from time immemorial', according to Hay, at the junction of the four Pallants, and was thus immediately outside the new house.[24] Henry was allowed to do this provided he set up 'a convenient shedd' in St Martin's Lane as an alternative market side.[25] Mary Sybella Peckham who was born in 1830 states in an account of her family that Henry had the cross removed 'because it got in the way of his coach'.[26] But getting rid of the crowds and clatter on market day - let alone the smell of the leather - was probably just as important to Henry, and just how important this was he may not have realised until he moved in. Henry's apothecary's bill has survived listing the purchases he made over a period of sixteen years.[27] The bill refers to him 'in ye Pallant' in June 1713, and it is probably safe to assume that this is about the time that he and Elizabeth took up residence in their new house.

Unfortunately there is no mention in the estimate of a fee to whoever drew up 'the London Modell', and at no time was he required to give his views on the cost of executing the design. Had he been well known, it seems improbable that the name would not have figured in the court proceedings. Sir John Summerson remarks that a London craftsman at that period could usually (if he were a mason, bricklayer or carpenter) make a plain 'draught' of a building.[28] In 1717 Henry Smart, the mason, gives his age as 'about 40'. At a time when the profession of architect was unknown, he was clearly able to plan and construct a house himself without supervision, and this what he initially agreed to do for Henry. What Smart received from Henry when the latter returned from London was not necessarily a working drawing but, since it had to be 'read' to Elizabeth, certainly a design.

Which buildings in London had fired Henry's imagination? It is not known whether he had visited London before his association with Elizabeth began, and if he had he is unlikely to have spent his time examining architecture. There

Facing page: Henry Peckham and his sister Judith, English School, c.1690. Oil on canvas, 41½ × 46½ in. Private Collection.

JUDITH PECKHAM.   HENRY PECKHAM, Esqr of Chichester
                   Born 1683. Died 1764.

35

is no doubt that she raised the sights of him and his family beyond the confines of Chichester; for instance, it must have been at her suggestion that Henry's sister, Anne, was apprenticed to a London milliner in January 1711.[29] And with Elizabeth, Henry would have seen the interior of a house such as 10 Soho Square whose lease she did not dispose of until just before the marriage. The majority of London houses at that time were confined for reasons of space to two or three bays in width. Elizabeth's house in Soho Square, of a spacious six bays in her time but originally built as two houses, had no influence on the design of Pallant House, although Henry was able to plan on similarly generous lines. He appears to have been attracted by a London style of building favoured by rich merchants among whom his wife's money enabled him to be numbered.[30] Unfortunately only a few examples of this style survive. The closest to Pallant House is probably Rutland Lodge at Petersham, originally two storeys in height (it is now three) with similarly elaborate brick decoration and large-scale doorway. There are also later examples still standing such as The Barons, Church Street, Reigate built by Richard Devon in 1721. Henry built in expensive red brick; his house has a fashionable parapet roof (obligatory in London after 1707) and modern sash-windows, though it is worth noting that Smart has placed these on the same plane as the brick face rather than recessing them by the four inches required by that time in London. Though this stipulation was not applicable to Chichester, it set a precedent which was soon followed by builders outside the capital. Many of the details of Pallant House are probably attributable to Smart, certainly the fine craftsmanship was entirely due to him and his team. Smart was the son of a bricklayer; he worked continuously from 1715 until 1730 for the Goodwood estate, and served as mayor of Chichester in 1751-2. He was buried in the cathedral cloisters in 1760.

There is no contemporary description of the furniture or decoration of the house in the Peckhams' day; the court proceedings refer to two chimneypieces Elizabeth had installed which were made up by Smart out of marble tables owned by her brother. Only the double portrait of Henry as a child depicted in classical dress with his sister Judith can be said with any reasonable degree of probability to have hung in the house in his time. Neither the painter nor the patron is known, but the sitters are identified by an old inscription on the canvas, and this is not incompatible with the dating of the work on stylistic grounds. No later painting of Henry Peckham has been discovered, but it is unlikely that certain features such as the high forehead, the full cheeks and the weak chin altered much as he grew older. When Elizabeth died in 1749 she left in her

A detail of the Adam-style 'Bonheur-de-Jour' in the Cabinet.

will a list of her most cherished possessions which she wished preserved for an infant great-nephew:

> My Buroe Dressing Table and Glass in my best chamber, my Green Bed in the fore Chamber with the Bolsters, Pillows, Bedstead, Curtains and Vallens and all things thereto belonging, and the Quilt upon the Bed I lye on, two Armed Chairs in the best Parlour that are noways broke, and my Mahogany Table and Mahogany sea chest.

That Elizabeth set great store by her household goods is evident, and the list though compiled years after she left Pallant House an indication of the care with which she would have attended to its furnishing. She also refers to her collection of books, including a large bible and a copy of a popular devotional work, *The Whole Duty of Man*.

Elizabeth, pious, domesticated and bookish, appears to have found life with Henry difficult once the challenge and excitement of building Pallant House was over. He fell into arrears with her pin money which would have curtailed her freedom, and he made no attempt to produce the accounts of her investments required by the terms of the marriage settlement. On 2 January 1716 Elizabeth's father, Charles Cutter, was buried at Ferring; later that spring she was happy

A small selection of the Geoffrey Freeman Collection of Bow porcelain. The Mongolian Prince and Princess (c1750), two shell salts (1747-50) and the beautifully crafted Handel watch-case, decorated with music and a figure of Time (1759), one of the finest products of the Bow factory. (By courtesy of Mrs. G. Freeman.)

enough to rebuild her kitchen at Pallant House. But by the end of the year she had left house and husband and, with the help of her brother-in-law, the Revd Serenus Barrett, Headmaster of Midhurst Grammar School, taken her woes to court. What prompted her to do so at that moment is unclear: we know there were aspects of Henry's business dealings she did not care for, but perhaps solicitude for her elderly father prevented her from leaving in his lifetime. Cutter did not officiate at his daughter's second marriage, and his intense distrust of Henry could hardly be made plainer in his will.(31)

The Victorian Kitchen, packed with the most up-to-date equipment of the time.

PECKHAM V. PECKHAM

To the court Elizabeth complains only of Henry's financial dishonesty. In her bill dated 24 November 1716, she alleges that Henry 'altered disposed & converted' for his own use the greater part of her £10,000, and, 'combineing & confederating himself with the United Company of Merchants of England trading to the East Indyes…in a secret & clandestine manner sold disposed & transferred several parts & parcells of the personal Estate aforesaid to & amongst themselves'[32]. Elizabeth asks the court to direct Henry to make good the articles of the marriage settlement, freeze the £2,000 of East India Company stock which was still intact, and pay the arrears of her pin money because the separation from Henry had left her destitute. Henry's reply to her bill is dated 14 February 1717. He begins by disputing the size of Elizabeth's fortune, estimating it at little more than £5,000 which he could account for with the expenditure of £3,000 upon Pallant House and the £2,000 East India stock in hand. He accuses Elizabeth of hiding some of her assets from him, and adds that he assumed during the building of Pallant House and for some considerable time afterwards that the house adequately fulfilled the demands of the settlement; and had he not felt this, he states, he would never have embarked upon it, Elizabeth knowing that he could not possible have paid the bills out of his own resources.

Henry also attacks Elizabeth personally, insisting that he had far more reason to complain of broken promises than she had, and refers to 'the uncandid & unfaire Treatment [he] hath already mett with…in almost every Step of his proceedings with her'. Most arrogantly and heartlessly Henry implies that only Elizabeth's fortune made her a desirable proposition as a wife, and adds that he would never have lavished gifts upon her before their marriage 'to the value of severall hundred pounds' had she been penniless; he speaks scathingly of her worldly wealth before she received her inheritance: two £50 bonds *which paid no interest.*

Their battle lasted four years. The court was satisfied that Henry had indeed expended £3,000 on Pallant House, but his diminution of Elizabeth's fortune was not accepted. As he could not produce the sum of £7,000 required for the two bequests in their respective wills a compromise was eventually struck. Henry was ordered to pay the arrears of the pin money and to provide a settlement of £3,500, if necessary from his own resources. The final agreement 'for putting an End to all Suits and Differences…and for setling…a Separate Maintenance' is dated 29 December 1720[33]. At Elizabeth's request £2,500 of this sum was spent on the purchase of the lease of Aldingbourne Farm. One further skirmish between the two is recorded. In 1723 Elizabeth was incensed to find that Henry had encouraged Dr Brune Bickley, a Chichester physician to whom she had lent £800, not to repay his debt[34]. As far as is known, Elizabeth remained in Chichester until her death in 1749. Her bequests included £50 to her goddaughter Mary, wife of Thomas Capell, the organist at the Cathedral, and eighteen pence a week to Jane Edwards 'whom I brought up' for as long as she is unmarried 'and keeps herself honest'. Her two principal legatees were John Staker, an infant grandson of John Albery's sister, Abigail, whose education she entrusted to Canon John Backshell of Chichester, and her kinsman, Edward Emily of New Inn, her brother's nephew. She left £5 each to Henry and his only surviving sister, Anne, to buy mourning rings, and by doing this hoped no doubt to ensure that neither could upset her will: Elizabeth remained mistrustful of Henry to the very last days of her life.

PHOTO HUGH PALMER

The Georgian-style walled garden, showing the standard honeysuckles and dwarf box hedging.

'LISBON' PECKHAM

We do not know why Henry Peckham acquired the name 'Lisbon' Peckham, although the late W.D. Peckham recalled a credible tradition in Chichester that he was a wine merchant. ('Lisbon' being the popular name in Henry's time for the wine of the province of Estremadura, shipped in large quantities to England from the Portuguese capital.) Alexander Hay states in his history of Chichester that Pallant House was built 'for the purpose of a custom-house', and if this is taken to mean a bonded warehouse, then we have not only a pointer to Henry's commercial interests, but also an explanation of the size of the cellar at Pallant House which is far larger than would be necessary for normal domestic purposes. Unfortunately no precise information has come to light about Henry's activities as a merchant.

We do know that Henry Peckham acquired the rudiments of a legal training in James Vavasor's office in Chichester, and that for about four years before his death in 1742, Richard Peckham of Nyton (whose portrait by Nazari hangs in Pallant House) employed Henry to manage his complex financial affairs.[35] Anne Morley of Strettington refers in her will of 1721 to 'that sume of money now remaining in the hands of Mr Lisbon Peckham' which suggests that Henry may also have acted for her in a similar capacity.[36] This mention of Henry as 'Lisbon' Peckham is the earliest so far discovered, though he was regularly referred to as such in the correspondence of the dukes of Newcastle and Richmond in the 1730s and 1740s.

The name 'Lisbon' might also imply that Henry was one of the self-styled Portugal merchants - based in London or at the British factories in Portugal - who were responsible for the great expansion of Anglo-Portuguese trade in the first half of the eighteenth century. By adopting it Henry would also have found a means of distinguishing himself from his cousin Henry Peckham, a mercer, who was a few years older and active from an early age in Chichester civic affairs.

Unfortunately Henry does not explain or justify the dealings with the East India Company which so distressed Elizabeth. We know of his visits to London: the Chancery Court proceedings refer to them during the building of Pallant House. It is worth recording too, that the church in which Henry and Elizabeth married stood on the corner of Threadneedle Street and Bishopsgate near the Company's

headquarters in Leadenhall Street. Henry's involvement with the Company may have stemmed from Sir Henry Peckham's day, but more likely Elizabeth's money was the key. Her brother's stock of £2,000 remained intact until she sold it herself in 1721.[37] This amount of stock would have set Henry at a considerable advantage; he would even have been eligible for election as one of the twenty-four directors, and certainly he would have had the entrée for trading within the Company.[38] The records show that up to a dozen part owners would fit out a ship and offer it to the Company to transport goods at stated rates, but very few of the owners are listed and when they were paid generally only the ship's name is given in the accounts.[39] This is the activity in which Henry is most likely to have participated. If money was lost, as Elizabeth's statement implies, there is no trace in the records of how this came about. Any legal action would be recorded in the minutes of the Court of Directors, so the Chancery Court could not have pursued her accusations against the Company.

It is also possible that the 'Lisbon' association came about through the East India Company, as many of the Company's ships put into Lisbon on their way to and from the East.[41] But Henry may have had more direct dealings. The Portugal trade in his day had been strenghtened by commercial treaties, the most famous of which was the Methuen Treaty of 1703 which established favourable terms for the import of English textiles into Portugal, and for Portuguese wines into England. This was negotiated by the British ambassador, John Methuen, with assistance from his son Paul, who succeeded his father at the Lisbon embassy.[42] It was, incidentally, Elizabeth's brother, Captain Cutter, who transported Paul Methuen from Genoa to Lisbon in 1706 to take up his new appointment, so there could, conceivably, have been some advantageous family link.[43]

A detail of the Drawing-Room showing the moulded cornice of around 1830-40 and the period-style brass picture-rails installed during restoration works.

In 1710 an Englishman in Portugal estimated that three-quarters of the wheat and all the dyed cloth were imported by English merchants.[44] In turn these merchants brought back gold and silver bullion, diamonds, tobacco and sugar (all initially from Brazil whose trade was required to pass through Lisbon), wine, oranges, lemons, figs, olives, olive oil and salt. Merchants in grain and textiles acted only as intermediaries, keeping neither stock nor warehouse; the wine trade was organized much as it is today, except that much of the Portuguese wine was shipped through provincial ports where import duties were less than those at London.[45]

Local wheat was the principal commodity shipped out of the ports of Chichester, Portsmouth and Southampton.[46] In 1720 wheat was exported from Portsmouth to Ireland, the Channel Islands, Spain, Portugal, Gibraltar, France, Sweden and Newfoundland, but as many of the port books are missing it is impossible to say whether Henry participated in this trade although we know he farmed at South Mundham until 1714.[47]

In his will Henry left a bequest of £100 to Henry Cox whom he describes as a ship carpenter in Portsmouth Dock, a connection which could have come about through ship-building or the timber trade. Daniel Defoe refers to the timber shipped down the Arun as being 'esteem'd the best' by the naval dockyards of which Portsmouth was the nearest to Chichester. Oak and other local timber was sent by ship from Shoreham, Arundel and Chichester principally to London, Chatham, Plymouth and Portsmouth, and softwood came from Scandinavia; the Chichester port book for 1716 records the import of 'wainscot boards' from Norway.[48] Also relevant here is a minute of a council meeting in Chichester of 1732 which states that Henry was given permission 'to take down & convert to his own use' two elm trees near the East Walls in return for six bottles of wine.[49] In the General Election campaign of 1741, the Opposition in Chichester - organised by Henry - surprised the Duke of Newcastle's agents by sending to London for a hogshead of shrub with which to woo the Chichester voters for the Tories.[50] Shrub was a mixture of rum and orange or lemon juice, and a hogshead was over fifty gallons. Perhaps it was not possible to find in Chichester so large a quantity of rum at a time when wine and very strong beer was the usual drink in the public houses. Henry's gesture certainly impressed his opponents even if it failed to secure extra votes for his party. Any potential supporter who claimed his quota of Henry's extravagant largesse would have been totally incapacitated; and if this was Henry's idea of reasonable drinking the thought occurs that the nickname 'Lisbon' might allude merely to an intemperate consumption of that most popular wine.

Henry Peckham is described as 'a noted manager for the Tory interest' in Chichester, in a letter of 1733 by an agent of the Duke of Newcastle, Secretary of State for the Southern Department and the most powerful magnate in Sussex.[51] The Duke was a supporter of the Whig administration of Sir Robert Walpole; the Duke of Richmond, who had considerable influence in and about Chichester, described his own attachment to the Whigs as 'steady & firm', and his friendship with Newcastle as 'inviolable'.[52] For some reason Henry set himself the task of mobilising opponents to this formidable team. Old loyalties and family connections possibly played a part in his choice. Thomas Carr, who came so swiftly to Henry's aid when as a child he was threatened with the loss of his inheritance, was elected Tory MP for Chichester in 1708, and two of the kinsmen Henry mentions in his will, Thomas D'Oyly and Thomas Ludgater, both voted for the Opposition in 1734.[53] Whig attempts between 1729 and 1736 to raise the duty on wines and spirits, and the shadow of Walpole's attempt to place a tax on commodities which, though abandoned, hung over the election campaign of 1733/4, were all incompatible with Henry's presumed interests as a merchant.[54]

Henry makes a first appearance in the Newcastle correspondence as manager for Colonel Thomas Yates who stood unsuccessfully for Chichester in the Tory interest at a by-election in 1733.[55] The Duke of Richmond was told that'whoreing' cost Yates the election, although he won in the following year.[56] In the canvass for the county contest of 1734, Newcastle was informed that 'Mr Parke & Mr Peckham are indefatigable ag[ains]t us', Parke being a canon residentiary in the cathedral whom the Duke of Richmond once accused of harbouring Jacobite sympathies.[57] With two good candidates, Sir Cecil Bysshopp of Parham and John Fuller, the Sussex Opposition was a credible force. Bysshopp, accompanied by Henry, canvassed among the Chichester freeholders, and Henry also went to Arundel with Fuller, whose campaigning zeal it was said, 'made him caress even the meanest of the people, so they could roar out, "No excise" '.[58] Although Bysshopp and Fuller lost the election, they received a respectable share of the vote. But by 1740 when the question arose of selecting candidates for the General Election of the following year, it was apparent that support for the Opposition had dwindled. Bysshopp announced that he would not stand, whereupon Henry and Parke angrily accused him to his face of deserting their cause. Newcastle's agent reported that Bysshopp 'seem'd to take what had been said to him...very ill'.[59] The sole Opposition candidate, Samuel Medley, proved to be a most uninspiring choice, and neither the hogshead of shrub nor Henry's efforts as a canvasser had much effect on the Chichester voters. An epidemic of smallpox claimed Medley's life shortly before the election so his popularity was never put to the test, but it also carried away one of the successful Whig candidates ten days after, leaving the survivors to face a by-election. In June 1741 Henry was seen at a cricket match at Stansted in the company of the new candidate, Thomas Sergison of Cuckfield. Later that month Sergison held a party for his supporters at the Dolphin, but, despite the fact that he had visited the house of every freeholder in Chichester, the attendance barely reached thirty. This was all very discouraging, and as polling day drew nearer Henry was heard to declare that 'it was a lost game'. The Duke of Richmond passed on this comment to Newcastle, adding with satisfaction, 'All this wee know very well, butt I am glad to hear that Lisbon Peckham say'd it'.[60] In the end Sergison took the unanimous advice of his friends and withdrew his candidacy. Some years later, in 1746, the Duke of Richmond's nephew, Lord Bury, was elected MP for Chichester at a by-election. Reporting the success to Newcastle, Richmond wrote, 'Ld Bury was chose...without opposition...when he went round the town...even Lisbon Peckham told him, not only now butt at the next Genll Election he might depend upon his vote, & what interest he could make for him.'[61] In view of this change of heart, it is less surprising to find that one of Henry's last appearances as a member of the Chichester Corporation was at a ceremony in 1756 welcoming to the city a Hanoverian prince, the Duke of Cumberland, the brutal suppressor of the Jacobite Rising of 1745.[62]

HENRY PECKHAM AND
THE CORPORATION OF CHICHESTER

Henry Peckham's connection with the Corporation dates from 11 January 1717 when he was nominated and subsequently chosen to act as customer of the port of Chichester for the year.[63] He was admitted to the freedom of the city in the form of admission to the merchants' guild, and as such became a member of the common council.[64] Later that year, in September, he was elected bailiff, a title he retained by custom for the rest of his life although his duties were confined to a period of a year.[65] Despite attempts to advance himself in the hierarchy of the corporation, he never succeeded in becoming an alderman, let alone the mayor - although, uniquely in his time, he was nominated and rejected on four occasions.

In 1722 he stood with his cousin Henry, the mercer, but when the clerk opened the ballot box it was discovered that every single vote had been cast for the mercer. In the following year Henry was nominated by this cousin, but the nomination was objected to by some of the aldermen and was not allowed to proceed. Henry was not deterred by these setbacks, and in 1725 his name was put forward once more this time by the incumbent mayor, John Harris, who had both his candidates rejected, though later, as a compromise, Henry's name was allowed to stand. He lost by a margin of twenty-two to thirteen. His last attempt was in 1726, but on this occasion his opponent Benjamin Covert was elected by a large majority. Thereafter Henry must have realised that either his politics, or his personality, or aspects of his past disqualified him from consideration in the eyes of the majority of the corporation.[66] Henry's politics were possibly the most important of these considerations, and, as we know from his activities after 1733, he was never afraid to profess his beliefs, however unfashionable they may have been. Certainly Covert was proposed in 1733 as a 'counterbalance' to Henry in managing the Duke of Newcastle's political interests in Chichester, and Henry Peckham, the mercer, voted for the Duke's candidate in 1734.[67]

The divisive nature of political and religious debate at this period is worth noting here. James Spershott, a Chichester joiner born in 1710, wrote that 'the persecutions and furious contentions about religion' which were a feature of the latter part of the seventeenth century, 'were not forgot nor worn out' until far into the eighteenth, and, he added, 'the several denominations were too apt to look with a disrespectful eye on each other and stigmatize one another with characters of reproach as high church, and low church, Whigs and Tories, Jacobites, &c.'[68] Nothing we know of Henry suggests that his behaviour or his political affiliations would have appealed to the 'great many sober religious persons', described by Spershott, who packed the churches and meeting houses of Chichester. Although the rich merchants of Chichester adopted a very puritanical outlook towards the trappings of wealth, Henry by contrast had no such reservations: his grand new house in a city of 'very mean appearance' must have aroused mixed feelings. Spershott recalled that in his youth no more than three coaches were in private hands excluding the bishop's, and although we do not know for certain that Henry and Elizabeth possessed one, Peckham family tradition suggests they did.[69] If Henry's way of life caused resentment, his attitude towards Elizabeth must have been widely deplored. When we add to these the arrogance he displayed in court, and the insolence which shocked Sir Ceil Bysshopp, his rejection as mayor is hardly a surprise.

Not much can be deduced from the pattern of Henry's attendance at council meetings, but he is present, for instance, regularly in 1737, 1738 and 1742 but only once in each of the years 1739, 1740 and 1741. After 1742 his attendance was very sporadic; in the 1760s he makes just two appearances, on one occasion to greet the young Duke of York (a brother of George III) and, for the last time, in 1763, when Lord George Lennox was elected mayor.[70]

One other reference is worth recalling. 'Mr Peckham' appears in the churchwarden's accounts of the parish of St Peter the Less in 1734, settling a bill for 6s.6d. 'for work done at puting up the Dragon'.[71] This dragon was a celebrated weathervane which stood on the tower of the church (demolished in 1957) in which Henry was baptised.

LAST DAYS

It is not known how long Henry Peckham remained at Pallant House. The apothecary's bill refers to him in 1729 'in ye Pallant'; and the inhabitant's list of 1740 shows a Peckham in that part of Chichester with a household of four.[72] But the house is not mentioned in his will.[73] This was written a few days before he died on 15 May 1764 at the age of eighty. He bequeathed a life interest in property in Middleton and in East Street, Chichester to his kinsman Thomas Ludgater, to go subsequently to his cousin Harry Peckham, a promising Oxford undergraduate (later Recorder of Chichester). Henry's cousin Mary Levitt (also a grandchild of Sir Henry Peckham) was to receive property in North Mundham which on her death was to go to her son, the Revd Thomas D'Oyly, a former chancellor of Chichester Cathedral who lived for some years at the house in West Street built by John Edes.[74] Henry also remembered his two servants, Mary Hammond being left £50 'on account of her long and faithful service and the great care she has taken of me particularly during illness', and Sarah Catchlove £4. His executor and residuary legatee was his cousin, the Revd Harry Peckham, vicar of Amberley.

Henry Peckham was buried in the church of All Saints in the Pallant. A ledger stone in the chancel commemorated him and his sister Anne who died in 1751; these inscriptions, no longer legible, were recorded by Sir William Burrell.[75]

SIBYLLA JANE FLOWER

ACKNOWLEDGEMENTS

The research for this essay was begun under the tutelage of my cousin, the late W.D. Peckham, Honorary Archivist to the Dean and Chapter of Chichester. Christopher Whittick of the East Sussex Record Office helped with the search of the Chancery Court records in the Public Record Office, and Timothy and Alison McCann advised on many aspects of West Sussex history and commented on the first draft of the text. I would also like to thank A.S. Adams of the Middle Temple for information about Sir Henry Peckham; H.M. Colvin CVO, CBE; K.W.E. Gravett; Dr T.P. Hudson; Roy R. Morgan for details of the career of Henry Smart; and Mrs V.M. Tritton for giving me access to the archives at Parham, and permitting me to quote from them.

Notes

1 For the genealogy of the West Sussex Peckham family, see W.D. Peckham, 'Pedigrees' (manuscript and typescript, in author's possession).

2 Suss. Rec. Soc., xix, 145; J.S. Cockburn (ed.), *Calendar of Assize Records, Sussex Indictments Elizabeth I*, London, 1975, pp. 385, 394, 396-7, 403, 404, 411, 419.

3 Basil Duke Henning, *The History of Parliament, The House of Commons 1660-1690*, III, London, 1983, pp. 214-5; Anthony Fletcher, *A County Community in Peace and War: Sussex 1600-1660*, London, 1975, pp. 220, 295, 301, 302.

4 He was assessed for thirteen fire hearths and stoves in 1670, William Durrant Cooper, 'Former Inhabitants of Chichester', Suss. Arch. Coll. 24 (1872), p. 79; PCC 83 Pye.

5 Charles Dalton (ed.), *English Army Lists and Commission Registers, 1661-1714*, I, London, 1892, pp. 220, 237.

6 Public Record Office, C10 515/63.

7 West Sussex Record Office, Raper Box AK.

8 PRO, C6 549/120.

9 Chichester Dean's Ct., wills, VI, 15, dated 18 Mar 1687, proved 18 Aug 1705; PRO, C9 425/152; Thomas Carr 1658-1721, son of Alan Carr of the Middle Temple, was MP for Chichester, 1708-10.

10 PRO, C11 293/5, 971/31, 1166/72; C33 330/22, 330/130.

11 PRO, C10 515/63. Katherine was the widow of Stephen Penford, mayor of Chichester in 1669-70 anmd 1677-8. Her grandson, Thomas Ludgater, was a close friend and legatee of Henry Peckham.

12 PRO, C11 1166/72.

13 PRO, C11 293/5. As far as is known Joan remained at the farm until her death about 1726 when it passed to her son-in-law, William Peachey, WSRO, Raper Box AK.

14 Guy, Bishop of Chichester to the Archbishop of Canterbury, 13 March 1680, Ms. Tanner, 149, fol. 86b. Bodleian Library, Oxford.

15 Martha Cutter, daughter of William Wade, rector of Broadwater c.1669-1714, was buried at Broadwater, MI. No children of the marriage to Cutter are registered at Ferring or Broadwater.

16 I have here assumed that Susan (named after her mother) was the eldest (bapt. 1664).

17 Arundel PR, burial 8 May 1701, John, son of 'John Allbury of Houghton'.

18 PCC 354 Lisle.

19 John Charnock, *Biographia Navalis*, III, London, 1795, p. 95. His will, PCC 106 Smith.

20 PRO, C11 293/7; C33 332/187.

21 Ms. Tanner, 149, fol. 145, Bodleian Library, Oxford.

22 PRO, C7 230/68.

23 PRO. C11 2334/11.

24 Alexander Hay, *The History of Chichester,* Chichester, 1804, p. 190.

25 Hay, op.cit., pp. 189-90; Minute Book of Common Council of Chichester 1685-1738, C/1, f.255.

26 Mary Sybella Peckham MSS., Vol. 3, p. 41.

27 Private Collection, Chichester.

28 John Summerson, *Georgian London*, London, 1945, p. 53.

29 'The Apprentices of Great Britain 1710-1762', typescript, Society of Genealogists.

30 Tunstall Small and C. Woodbridge, *Houses of the Wren and early Georgian Periods*, London, 1928.

31 Chichester Cons.Ct.wills 32, 32.

32 PRO, C11 293/7.

33 WRSO, Add. Ms. 5112.

34 PRO, C11 52/4.

35 Hay, op.cit., p. 190.

36 PRO, C11 1166/72; C12 297/16; Chichester Cons.Ct.wills 33, 30.

37 India Office Records, L/AG/14/5/4.

38 W.R. Scott, *The Constitution and Finance of English, Scottish and Irish Joint-Stock Companies to 1720,* II, Cambridge, 1910, p. 180.

39 IOR, E/1/4, ff. 99, 100, 101, 102 (1712).

40 IOR, L/AG/14/5/3.

41 e.g. IOR, E/1/8, ff. 132, 133, 162.

42 H.V. Livermore, *A New History of Portugal*, Cambridge, 1966, p. 217-8.

43 Charnock, op.cit., p. 95.

44 Carl A. Hanson, *Economy and Society in Baroque Portugal, 1668-1703*, London, 1981, p. 274.

45 H.E.S. Fisher, *The Portugal Trade. A Study of Anglo-Portuguese Commerce 1700-1770*, London, 1971, pp. 17, 18, 19, 20, 24, 32, 56-7, 63, 65, 78-9, 92.

46 John H. Farrant, 'The Seaborne Trade of Sussex, 1720-1845', SAC, 114 (1976), pp. 103-4.

47 PRO, E190 861/2.

48 Farrant, op.cit., pp. 108-9; PRO, E190 810/27.

49 Minute Book, C/1, f. 390.

50 W. Battine to Duke of Newcastle, East Marden, 26 Oct. 1740, British Library, Add. Ms. 32, 695, ff. 343-4.

51 Fra.Allen to Robert Burnett, Chichester, 27 Aug. 1733, BL, Add. Ms. 32, 688, f. 190.

52 [Charles, 2nd] Duke of Richmond to Sir Cecil Bysshopp, 25 Aug. 1733, Parham Papers, XLVII, 'Letters 1708-1921'. Addenda, Add. 158.

53 Poll Book for county election [1734], BL, Add. Ms. 33, 059B.

54 *Political History of England*, IX, pp. 344-5, 350-2.

55 Fra. Allen to Robert Burnett, Chichester, 7 Sept. 1733, BL, Add. Ms. 32, 688, f. 285.

56 Timothy J. McCann (ed.), 'The Correspondence of The Dukes of Richmond & Newcastle 1724-50', SRS 73(1984), p. 52.

57 Thomas Ball to Duke of Newcastle, Chichester, 4 Nov. 1733, BL, Add. Ms. 32, 689, f. 9; L.P. Curtis, *Chichester Towers*, New Haven and London, 1966, p. 29.

58 G.H. Nadel, 'The Sussex Election of 1741', SAC, 91 (1953), p. 465.

59 J[ohn] Jewkes to Duke of Newcastle, Petworth, 3 Sept. 1740, BL, Add. Ms. 32, 694, f. 571.

60 McCann, op.cit., pp. 63, 66, 77.

61 McCann, op.cit., pp. 229-30.

62 Minute Book of Common Council of Chichester 1738-1783, C/2, f. 81v.

63 Minute Book, C/1, f. 280.

64 I am grateful to Mr T. McCann for this information.

65 Minute Book, C/1, f.285.

66 Minute Book, C/1, ff. 310, 320, 349, 353-4.

67 Thomas Ball to Revd Dr [Isaac] Maddox, 3 Oct. 1733, BL, Add. Ms. 32, 688, f. 447; Poll Book for county election [1734], BL, Add. Ms. 33, 059B.

68 Francis W. Steer (ed.), *The Memoirs of James Spershott*, Chichester, 1962, pp. 14-15.

69 Steer, op.cit., p. 13; MSP 3, p. 41.

70 Minute Book, C/2, f. 114v, 120v.

71 Lindsay Fleming, *The Little Churches of Chichester*, Bognor Regis, 1957, p. 4.

72 WSRO, Lists and Indexes, No. 1, 1954.

73 Chichester Cons.Ct.wills 37, 139.

74 WSRO, Add. Ms. 11, 790; D'Oyly lived at the John Edes House, see Francis W. Steer, *The John Edes House, West Street, Chichester*, Chichester, 1968, p. 8; see also, William D'Oyly Bayley, *A Biographical, Historical and Heraldic Account of the House of D'Oyly*, London, 1845, pp. 79-81.

75 BL, Add. Ms. 5699, f. 165.

Facing page: The front entrance of Pallant House as it was in 1912. Little has changed except for the position of the railing up the front steps, the removal of the little canopy over the fanlight and the alteration of the fanlight itself. The front door, still bearing its number nine in this photograph, is now hinged on the other side.

CHRONOLOGY - PALLANT HOUSE AND CHICHESTER

1683 : Henry Peckham born, the eldest son of John and Joan Peckham of Boxgrove.

1684 : Visit to Chichester of Sir Christopher Wren.

1696 : John Edes House, West Street, Chichester, completed.

1699 : Stockbridge House, Chichester, built for Francis Sone, tanner, by John Lilliott.

1711 : Henry 'Lisbon' Peckham marries Elizabeth Albery (née Cutter), in London 20th May.

1712/14 : Pallant House built by Henry Smart Snr. for Henry and Elizabeth Peckham.

1713 : Henry Peckham ordered to pay ground rent for his 'new buildings'.

1716 : Kitchen extension at Pallant House demolished and rebuilt.

1720 : Separation settlement between Henry and Elizabeth Peckham. Elizabeth had probably moved out of Pallant House by this time.

1733 : Council Chamber, North Street, Chichester, built to the design of Roger Morris.

1741 : "Madame" Peckham living in Little London, Chichester.

1749 : Death of Elizabeth Peckham.

1755 : A Henry Peckham listed as living in St. Martin's parish.

1764 : Death of Henry 'Lisbon' Peckham. Buried All Saints in the Pallant 18th May.

1774 : Footwalks in streets and lanes of Chichester all paved.

1781/2 : Assembly Rooms, Chichester, built behind Council Chamber.

1782 : Hon. Coote Molesworth recorded as owner and occupier of Pallant House.

1786 : Mrs. Hannah Luxford, widow, known to be owner and occupier of Pallant House.

1793 : Pallant House left by Mrs. Luxford to her sisters, Frances, Dorothy, Martha and Abigail Jordan (or Jardine).

1795 : Pallant House sold to Joseph Godman, yeoman, for £1,400.

1799 : Pallant House insured for £800.

1808 : The Butter Market, North Street, by John Nash, opened for business.

The Drawing-Room as it was in 1980, before restoration works began.

1812 : (approx) Present extension adjoining the Kitchen built. (Transferred to ownership of Joseph Godman 1838).

1840 : Death of Joseph Godman. Mary, his widow, continues in occupation of Pallant House.

1846 : The railway comes to Chichester.

1851 : Pallant House bought from Joseph Godman Jnr. by William Duke, solicitor, for £1,500.

1896 : Death of William Duke; Pallant House passes to Augusta Mary Watson, his daughter.

1904 : Pallant House sold to Edward Hawes, of Richmond, Surrey, for £1,500.

1913 : Pallant House sold to Mrs. Ida von Grundherr, also for £1,500. "Pallant House" as a name first used officially.

The Drawing Room, with paintings from the permanent collection of Modern British art.

1914	:	Mr. von Grundherr arrested by the War Office, and Pallant House searched by the military.
1919	:	Pallant House re-possessed by Edward Hawes and sold to the Westhampnett Rural District Council for £1,600.
1934 & 1966	:	Extensions to the rear of the house, giving a Council Chamber and other facilities.
1979	:	Pallant House vacated by Chichester District Council to allow its restoration, and the acceptance of Dean Hussey's collection.
1982	:	Pallant House Gallery opened to the public under the joint administration of the District Council and the Friends of Pallant House (formed 1979).
1985	:	Transfer to Charitable Trust status.
	:	Death of Walter Hussey.
1987	:	Completion of second phase of restoration.
1989	:	Receipt of Charles Kearley Bequest.
1992	:	Third phase of restoration to complete rooms in the main body of the house.

THE GARDEN

It was not until 1982 that attention was turned towards the garden at Pallant House which was designed by Claud Phillimore assisted by Edward Rutherfoord and planted under the aegis of Mrs. Stella Palmer. They began with few advantages, for the site was little more than an irregularly L-shaped backyard, the truncated remains of a larger garden which in the eighteenth century had stretched both to the north and east. There were no mature trees and the area had been encroached upon by office extensions which gave no thought to their effect either on the garden area or how they impaired appreciation of the fine rear façade of the house.

The area, therefore, presented many problems in terms of evoking a town garden of the period; the style would have been formal, calling for vistas and perspectives and above all symmetry. What sort of garden would have been here in 1713? At that date it was usual for the public rooms of a house to be at the front and the private ones at the rear. From these windows, away from the hurly burly and noise of the street, the owners would look down on their garden whose strongest emphasis would have been on geometric pattern to be viewed from above with an abundant use of clipped evergreens, yews, box and phillyrea, gravel walks and walls for espaliered fruit trees. There would usually have been a raised terrace next to the house or at the far end of the garden and an abundance of plants in containers, tulips in spring and, in summer, the newly imported 'exotics' from the Americas, the West Indies and the Cape of Good Hope. Those which were tender would have been taken in for the winter.

There is no such thing as an accurate re-creation of a period garden on the basis of the availability of plant varieties alone. An evocation is possible and this is what has successfully been attempted here, for the design had also to cope with the problems of low maintenance and public use. The important decision was to formalise the space by superimposing a rectangle onto the area which contains twelve beds. This imposition of symmetry is enhanced by the introduction of the correct gravel walks. Any reader of Celia Fiennes' travels will know her keen appreciation of "fine gravel walks".

The beds are correctly defined by wooden planks set into the earth. The three near the house are planted with roses. The explosion in rose varieties only came late in the century, so that here there are three beautiful old ones: the pink damask 'Celsiana', ancient 'Alba', which appears in Dutch flower paintings, and the glorious scented 'Great Maiden's Blush', which was known as early as the fifteenth century.

The planting of the rest of the beds pinpoints the problems of re-creation, for they are planted in profusion. How dull, however, the effect would be if they had been correctly planted with each flower three feet from its neighbour, particularly when the beds are only four feet square. Their geometry is emphasised by box edging with cones at the corners and in the central beds by the introduction of standard honeysuckles to give height. Each bed is scatter planted with historic flowers. These include dianthus, of which were was already a huge number of varieties by the close of the sixteenth century.

Authentic varieties do not survive but what is available can be matched to those that appear in pictures. From the early period too there is *cardamine trifolia* (Lady's smock), *Catananche caerulea* (Cupid's dart) and *Allium moly* (Gerard's "golden garlicke"). From the eighteenth century new plants from China, Japan, Russia and the United States: *aquilegeia alpina* and *viridiflora, penstemon barbatus, viola cornuta, campanula carpatica* to name but a few.

In this way the garden at Pallant House, with its strong architectural structure and its delightful seasonal planting, acts as an inspiration to anyone with a small house of the period to embark on planting one complimentary to its architecture.

ROY STRONG

Lot 1.

THE VERY VALUABLE — FREEHOLD

PRIVATE RESIDENCE

WITH GARDEN AND STABLING,

SITUATE

At the Corner of the North and East Pallants, Chichester.

Believed to have been designed and built by SIR CHRISTOPHER WREN. It is most substantially built of Red Bricks highly ornamented, and standing at the junction of the four Pallant Streets, which is a favourite neighbourhood for residents. It has a pleasant open aspect, and is approached from the street by broad Stone Steps, having a stone Forecourt enclosed by Ornamental Iron Railings with Brick Pillars for the Gateway surmounted by Dodo birds,

IT CONTAINS—

In the Basement—Spacious Cellarage, divided into Wine Cellar, fitted with Three Bins, Beer Cellar, and Coal and Wood Cellars.

On the Ground Floor—Lofty Entrance Hall, 33ft. by 14ft. 6in. ; Library, 16ft. 6in. by 12ft. by 12ft. high ; Drawing Room, 18ft. by 19ft. by 12ft. high, opening by Folding Doors to the Dining Room, 15ft 6in. by 16ft. ; Pantry ; Kitchen ; Scullery ; and W.C. ; with Two Rooms beyond, which have been used for Offices, but might be readily converted into a Housekeeper's Room and Second Kitchen.

The First Floor is approached by a spacious handsome Carved Oak Staircase, well-lighted by a large window, and contains—

Landing.
East Back Bedroom..........10ft. 6in. by 13ft. by 11ft. 6in. high.
South Front ditto............15ft. 6in. by 19ft. by 11ft. 6in. ,,
Middle ditto..................14ft. 6in. by 15ft. by 11ft. 6in. ,,
North Front ditto............17ft. 6in. by 12ft. by 11ft. 6in. ,,
West Back ditto ....16ft. 6in. by 18ft. by 11ft. 6in. ,,
And W.C., with Back Staircase.

The Bedrooms are all en suite, and communicate with each other.

On the Second Floor are Four Bedrooms and a large Room (15ft. 6in. by 23ft.), with Box Room adjoining, with Staircase leading to roof.

At the Back, with a Side Entrance from the East Pallant, is a good Garden, Conservatory, and Closet.

THE STABLING

Adjoining consists of Stable-yard, with Entrance from the East Pallant, 2-stalled Stable and Harness Room, with Loft over, and Chaise-house.

The above House is exceedingly well built and dry, and stands well up from the street, it was for many years the residence of the late William Duke, Esq., and possession will be given on completion of the purchase.

The Tenant's Fixtures, a Schedule of which will be produced at the sale, shall be taken to by the Purchaser, at the sum of £30 12s.

A sale notice of November 1896, when Wyatt's offered Pallant House for sale on behalf of the executors of William Duke.

59

APPENDIX 1

CITY MINUTE BOOK (C1)

p. 250   8th June 1713

"It is by this assembly ordered by the consent and agreement of Henry Peckham esq present that the ancient purpeture rent of [ ] pence payable for the Malthouse on the old foundations be from henceforth paid for the new buildings of the said Henry Peckham on the new foundation thereof in the Pallant which hath been altered to make the new building Square toward the South the increment thereby being much the same as before alike quantity of ground left out and taken in."

p.255   2nd March 1713 [1714]

"It is ordered and agreed that Henry Peckham esq may take down the Pallant Market Cross and convert the materials to his own use he setting up a convenient shed for the same use at the end of Mr. Smith's house in St. Martin's Lane in turn thereof and that Mr. William Castle do keep the key thereof."

APPENDIX 2

CHICHESTER, SUSSEX

To be SOLD by Private Contract, on or before March 25, 1782, A large, commodious, modern-built FREEHOLD BRICK DWELLING HOUSE, sashed, with an elegant Frontispiece, situate in the Pallant, Chichester, Sussex, in a genteel neighbourhood, and in possession of the Hon. Coote Molesworth, Esquire. The above premises stand elevated with an ascent of eight stone steps, enclosed with a wrought iron pallisade, eight feet from front.

The house consists of an elegant hall 40 feet long, 15 feet wide, 11 feet 10 inches high, wainscotted and papered. At the east end of the hall is a curious inlaid geometrical staircase of Norway oak, walls paper'd, enlightened by a large compass sash.

On the right of the entrance of the front door is a dining-room 19 feet long, 18 feet wide, 11 feet 10 inches high, wainscotted; the ceiling richly ornamented with paper machee, with an elegantly carved chimney-piece surrounding red marble jams, slab, &c.

Within this room is a drawing-room, 15 feet six inches long, 16 feet wide, 11 feet 10 inches high, finished as above (except the chimney-piece) with folding doors glazed, white marble chimney-piece and slab, with a closet on each side of the chimney.

Left of the front door is a parlour 18 feet long, 10 feet six inches wide, 11 feet 10 inches high, wainscotted, a convenient beaufet, with side-board &c. white marble chimney piece and slab.

Behind said room is a passage to the cellar, with large cupboards compleat, also the back stairs, 82 steps from the cellar floor to the top of the house. Going on is a servants hall, with grate fixed, with a pantry, and many other conveniences.

Behind the above is a large lofty kitchen, 17 feet nine inches long, 13 feet 10 inches wide, 13 feet high, sashed. Beyond is a wash house, brew house, pump, sink, &c. &c.

First floor. Left hand is a bed-chamber, wainscotted and paper'd on canvass, same dimensions as the Drawing room, with two closets, a marble chimney piece and slab, a neat grate and mantle piece.

Bed chamber over great parlour, same dimensions as ditto, marble chimney piece and slab, two closets, chamber neatly wainscotted, and papered on canvas.

Over part of the hall, in front, is a chamber 16 feet long, 14 feet eight inches wide, 11 feet 10 inches high, wainscotted, a stone chimney piece and slab, with folding glazed doors.

In front, the Green Chamber, wainscotted and paper'd, 18 feet long, 12 feet six inches wide, 11 feet 10 inches high, wood In the passage, to the back stairs is a large cupboard with shelves, doors, &c. compleat: a bed chamber sashed, chimney &c. within which is a convenient store-room with shelves. This bedchamber leads to a newly-built bed-chamber, paper'd, and sashed with Venetian shades, a neat stove-grate, Dutch tiles, stone chimney-piece and slab, two closets with shelves, drawers &c.

Two large one small garret in front, lumber-room, &c. with chimneys.

The above premises stand on seven well-built brick arches, whole height from floor to crown seven feet nine inches, which comprehends, first, a large cold pantry, plaistered and cieled, a large vault or cellar 36 feet long, 19 feet wide, a ditto with six brick wine bins with covers, &c. a ditto contains nine brick bins; with three arches for wood, &c. beside four vaults under the pavement.

Behind the house is a small walled garden with fruit trees, a green plat for drying cloaths, a footway paved to back entrance, a reservoir for rain water, containing about six hogsheads. Two conductors.

With the House will be sold a Piece of ground, held by lease under the Dean and Chapter of Chichester, renewable every twelve years, containing a stable yard, with a large new built brick and tiled building, containing two stables, three stalls each, a coach-house, a room over it, with substantial hay and straw lofts, a pump and well of excellent water, with a small garden planted with the best of fruit-trees walled in.

The whole of the above premises are in exceeding good repair.

For further particulars inquire of the Possessor, of Mr. John Drew, banker, at Chichester, or of Edward Pasod, upholder, cabinet-maker and auctioneer, Chichester, who will shew the premises.

HAMPSHIRE CHRONICLE
11th March 1782

This Indenture made the ... twenty fourth day of April One thousand nine hundred and nineteen Between Robert Porson Hawes of 7 Great Winchester Street in the City of London Solicitor hereinafter called the Vendor of the one part and The Westhampnett Rural District Council (hereinafter called the Purchasers) of the other part Whereas the Vendor is now seised in fee simple in possession free from incumbrances of the hereditaments hereinafter described and has agreed to sell the same to the Purchasers for the like estate in possession free from incumbrances at the price of One thousand six hundred Pounds Now this Indenture witnesseth that in pursuance of the said agreement and in consideration of the sum of One thousand Six hundred Pounds paid by the Purchasers to the Vendor (the receipt of which sum the Vendor hereby acknowledges) The Vendor as beneficial owner hereby conveys unto the Purchasers All that Freehold Messuage or Dwellinghouse stable and other buildings garden and yards thereto adjoining

An indenture of sale, tranferring Pallant House from Robert Hawes to the Westhampnett Rural District Council in April 1919 for £1,600. The plan shows the original extent of the garden and outbuilding.

64